TEACH
— *and* —
GROW RICH

Share Your Knowledge to Create Global Impact, Freedom and Wealth

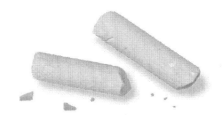

DANNY INY

Praise for the Author

"Danny... bring[s] a high level of insight, knowledge, and integrity to the online business world."

-**Guy Kawasaki**, Chief evangelist of Canva and author
of *The Art of the Start 2.0, The Art of Social Media,
Enchantment,* and nine other books

"Danny... is always full of energy, insight and passion for what people need to learn to truly be successful. ...I would not hesitate to recommend him or his company, based solely on his kindness, integrity and intensity."

-**Mitch Joel**, President and "Media Hacker"
at Mirum, the global digital marketing agency
operating in 20 countries, one of the top 100 online
marketers in the world, and author or best-sellers
Six Pixels of Separation and *CTRL ALT Delete*

"Danny... [is] a model of professionalism and quality. Anyone who's serious about online marketing should be following what... [he's] doing."

-**Michael Port**, world-renown speaker
and New York Times, Wall Street Journal,
and USA Today bestselling author of six books
including *Steal the Show* and *Book Yourself Solid*

"Danny... is a person who genuinely cares about others and is always working to make the world a better place and himself a better human being."

-**Srikumar Rao** is a TED speaker, best-selling author,
and creator of *Creativity and Personal Mastery* the
pioneering course that was among the most popular and
highest rated at many of the world's top business schools

"Danny Iny is revolutionizing internet marketing, courses, and all other forms of online education. His enlightened approach to generating a sustainable model for ongoing income and impact that is unmatched, and is rivaled only by the level of integrity that is present in everything that he does."

-**Hal Elrod**, #1 international bestselling author of
The Miracle Morning, a Hall of Fame business
achiever, and host of the *Achieve Your Goals* podcast

"Danny Iny... is the real deal."

-**Randy Gage**, member of the Speaker's Hall of Fame
and author of ten books translated into 25 languages,
including the New York Times bestsellers,
Risky Is the New Safe and *Mad Genius*

"When it comes to building your audience and designing online courses, Danny Iny is one of few experts I trust and personally follow - and someone I recommend all my customers follow as well."

-**Ryan Levesque**, entrepreneur, marketing strategist
and best-selling author of *Ask*

"We've all heard the old adage about "teaching a man to fish." I love Danny's ethic does because he doesn't believe in doing things any other way. A fantastic teacher, [and] a brilliant entrepreneur."

-**Sean Platt**, founder of the STERLING & STONE
STORY STUDIO, with six reader-loved imprints,
author and co-author of dozens of highly-rated novels,
as well as best-selling nonfiction

Praise from Readers
of the First Edition

"Another incredibly absorbing read from the mind of one of the smartest marketers on the planet, Danny Iny. One of the things I like most about Mr. Iny is his uncanny ability to identify certain key trends in the IM space early on and to articulate specific, actionable steps one can take in order to get ahead of the curve and flourish as an educator, entrepreneur, coach, trainer, author, speaker and/or marketer. He really nails it here when it comes to the importance of creating high-impact courses for one's followers and driving value into the customer equation at every possible stage. I can't recommend Danny's new book highly enough. It's a must-read. Period." -**Daniel Harris Ulin**

"This is the perfect book at the perfect time for me. Everything Danny talked about resonated with how I've been thinking lately. The question has always been, "How do I create value?" Danny supplies a big answer." -**George Mulraney**

"While reading this, I had several "Aha" moments. The truths are outlined clearly, and it is clear that Danny Iny has given this topic serious thought. His observations are keen, and I am excited to see what changes will come about as a result of this book. There is a saying that when the student is ready, the teacher will appear. Well, the teacher has appeared, and his name is Danny Iny!" -**E. N. Lumpkin**

"This is worth the time to read it a couple times. His logic is inescapable and his presence genuine. Thanks Danny." -**Doug McKee**

"This book gets 5 Stars! I enjoyed the enlightened (and confirming) information shared within these pages regarding the wave of the future for entrepreneurs who educate and engage with their students while building result-based online learning experiences. The TL;DR recap points were extremely beneficial for summing things up at the end of each chapter. This book gave me hope in future learning when it's done right! Thanks Danny :)" -**AJA Austin**

"Danny Iny talks the talk and walks the walk. This book opens the doors to the next big opportunity for the little guy, online education outside the traditional passive student model. Most of the education we encounter is based on an "empty" student being filled with knowledge from books or very rigid and one way teacher to classroom infodumps. The new paradigm of smaller is better, coupled with the reach of the internet, allows more interaction and the teaching of less mainstream topics that would not be viable otherwise. I think Danny is on to something yet again. Almost everyone has an expertise or interest they know more about than those starting to learn about it. The internet will allow you to find them, charge them, and teach them in a better fashion than the old paradigm would have allowed." -**Andres Pedraza**

"Danny Iny is the real deal! This book has opened my eyes to the true value and opportunity available today in online education. I'm excited and motivated for the part I can play in it. Beyond that, I've watched Danny practice what he's preaching in his own business... he truly does more than sell information. He educates and changes lives! Thank you Danny!" -**Mark Sieverkropp**

"FANTASTIC! I got the kindle version of this book with audible narrative. I am in the process of creating a website that teaches people how to play the piano and the importance of understanding the universal language of music. Danny Iny's book was exactly what I hoped it would be- information I can literally put into action. There is no padding or fluff in this book, which I find extremely refreshing. I am one tough customer- not easy to impress. I enjoyed listening to it and have done so several times! The book is written with the utmost of integrity and points out the intrinsic value of education." -**Katherine**

"Really enjoyed the book. Forget what you think about information and think education in a big way. Danny gives entrepreneurs a new lens to look through to see the world of online products. Required reading for aspiring entrepreneur educators!" -**Paul McGuire**

"If you are interested in creating an online course, please read Danny's book. I am a cautionary tale of what can happen when you do not follow Danny's proven plan in creating, marketing, and selling online courses. A little over a year ago I hired a company to help me create my first online course. Unfortunately, this company (though well-intentioned) had NO idea how to create, market, and sell online course. The end result is I committed every mistake Danny mentions in his book and waisted a lot of time, energy, and money. In reading Danny's book, I kept finding myself saying, "Yes! I should have done that!" when I was making my first course. Danny's book is an easy-to-read treasure trove of how to succeed in the very exciting field of online course creation. I highly recommend it for everyone seriously considering creating an online course." -**Michael Veltri**

"TEACH AND GROW RICH provides a thought-provoking perspective at the current state of online education, and suggests the path that's most likely to offer opportunities for entrepreneurs in the future. At a practical level, it offers a roadmap for conceptualizing, developing, and launching an online course in a way that increases its value for students/customers. This book has made me rethink the way I design and market online courses, and I would recommend it to anyone involved in -- or interested in becoming involved in -- online education." -**Traveling_Jane**

TEACH
and
GROW RICH

Share Your Knowledge to Create Global Impact, Freedom and Wealth

DANNY INY

TEACH AND GROW RICH:

Share Your Knowledge to Create Global Impact, Freedom, and Wealth

by Danny Iny

ISBN 13: 978-1541232518

Dedication to the 1st Edition:

This book is dedicated to my students.

*Each and every one of you is committed to creating
a better life for yourself and your family, by making
a positive impact on the world around you.*

*Your vision and dedication inspires and
motivates me to do the work that I do.*

So thank you – onward, and upward!

Dedication to the 2nd Edition:

*I sometimes say that business is
about more than just making money,
it's about finding a sustainable way to make
the impact that you care about making.*

*Like any parent, I want to leave for my children
a world that is better, happier, and more prosperous
than the one that I inherited from my parents...
and if each person who knows something that
can benefit someone else is empowered to
share that knowledge, it just might happen.*

*My hope is that this book can be the
first domino in that ripple of change.*

For my children, and for all of our children.

Table of Contents

Foreword:
If It Worked for Me...

In March of 2015, my business life changed forever. And it's all due to Danny Iny and the Mirasee team.

But let me step back for a moment.

In 2005, I opened a very traditional public relations firm. We excelled at media relations, event planning, reputation management, and crisis communications. I grew up in a large PR firm, whose framework I initially adopted into my own business, despite knowing it was broken. It was what I knew, but at the same time, I was frustrated by the lack of ability the industry had (and still has) to effectively move a business forward and I wanted to find a better way.

We began to test different theories, first on ourselves, and then implemented with clients. And, as the digital web began to enter the foray—and along with it came data—we discovered a way to measure public relations efforts to cold, hard cash.

At the same time, we launched a blog called Spin Sucks that was built simply to see if this blogging thing would make sense for clients. What we didn't expect was for it to take off, but it did, growing to become the world's leading PR blog.

We realized the PR industry very badly needed professional development and online training, both to master modern PR and measure PR efforts to real business goals. We saw a huge need and we aimed to fill it with a membership site.

In 2011, we launched that very thing and were met with crickets. It was a complete and utter disaster. Not one person signed up to take online training through Spin Sucks. It was devastating and expensive, and left us gun shy. But, I licked my wounds and set it aside while I focused on other things. I wrote a couple of books, went on the speaking circuit, and continued to build an agency that evolved from public relations to digital marketing.

And then Danny came along.

As I relayed my story of the membership site and how I didn't think the PR industry was primed to pay for professional development, he looked me straight in the eye and said, "I can help you."

I kind of poo-poo'd him. After all, we had tried it and it had failed. In fact, when my second book was published, the number of people who asked me for a free copy was astounding. If they weren't willing to ante up $20 for a book, I just knew they weren't going to buy anything more expensive. And it was our fault. For nearly 10 years, we primed our readers that everything we produced was free to them. Other than the failed membership site and two books, we'd never asked them to pay for anything.

With just a few tweaks to what we were already doing, a clearly-defined process, some goals, and a HUGE dose of confidence, Danny got us back on track. Later in 2015, we launched a mastermind group for PR firm owners and we piloted an online course. It was crazy successful!

Going into 2016, we knew we wanted to up the ante and, under Danny's tutelage, we did. As of this writing—at the end of 2016—we have one full mastermind group and a second one launching for PR managers and directors. We also have two successful full-blown courses. The goals for 2017 are even more lofty and my team and I have the confidence to blow through them because of Danny's help.

Every business owner looks for a return-on-investment on the money they spend. With Danny, our return was 1,500 percent. Not only did we make back the money we'd invested in him, we even hired two full-time people to work on the revenue-generating side of Spin Sucks. We did all the work, of course, but we never would have even tried had it not been for that fateful meeting in March of 2015.

As you traverse this book and think about how you can implement Danny's teachings in your business, my wish for you is that you have crazy success. If you pay really close attention to what Danny is teaching you, I promise you, you will have that experience.

Gini Dietrich
CEO, Arment Dietrich
Founder and author, Spin Sucks

Tale of an Unlikely Educator (Preface to the Second Edition)

I've never liked going out and partying late into the night... especially not on New Year's Eve. I'm not a fan of how much more expensive everything is; I don't enjoy being awake past the time when I would have preferred to be asleep; and I don't have patience for the crazy traffic jams caused by everyone rushing home minutes after midnight. More than any of that, I don't like the symbolism of starting the new year feeling tired, sluggish, and hungover. So I've always skipped the parties, gone to bed early, and started the new year fresh and energetic, while most of my friends were still sleeping.

That's what the morning of January 1, 2010 looked like for me. While the sun was still rising, I was up and out the door for a walk in the chilly Montreal winter. I contemplated the last few years, which had been one of the roughest periods of my life. The startup that I had put everything into had imploded with the crashing markets. Rather than tell my investors (who were friends and family) that their money was gone, I had taken the losses on myself, and walked away from it all with over a quarter of a million dollars of personal debt. And while all this was happening, my relationship with my then fiancée worked its way to a messy and painful end.

I don't know which was harder: getting over the breakup, or moving past the crater of entrepreneurial failure. I had to do both, of course, and by the start of 2010, I was feeling cautiously optimistic about the future. On the personal side, I had finally moved past the stage of acute heartbreak, and was only months away from meeting the woman who would later become my wife (though of course, I didn't know it yet). My work life was looking up, too; after my company collapsed, I rebuilt my consulting practice, and was doing well enough that I could stop worrying about making ends meet. It had taken years, but finally I had moved past the point of crisis.

Even so, when I looked at the different variables at play in my life, the math didn't seem to add up. In one column was the life I knew I had within me to live; debt paid off and maybe even some savings, time and resources to care for my family, freedom to take an occasional vacation, and work that makes a difference in the world. In other words, my personal manifestation of the impact, freedom, and wealth that many of us aspire to achieve. In the other column was a sharp contrast: a mountain of debt that I was ever so slowly paying off, prices that I believed I could reasonably charge for my time, excessive hours that I was working, the drudgery of working with clients I didn't love (and occasionally couldn't stand) just so I could pay the bills, a bone-wearying lack of down-time... and most importantly, the gnawing feeling that I was destined to play a bigger game, if I could only find a way to do it.

Drudgery		Impact
Time for Money	≠	Freedom
Debt		Wealth

That was seven years ago. Since then, my life has changed enormously, and for the better. I'm privileged to work with and support thousands of the world's most innovative online entrepreneurs, and I'm grateful for the financial returns that my work provides. My debt is paid off. I travel the world, and share my very rewarding work and life with my wife, who is also my business partner and best friend. This year, while I was tired and sluggish when I crawled out of bed on New Year's Day, the responsible parties weren't late nights or alcohol, but rather the antics of my two wonderful kids.

The path from there to here wasn't anything resembling a straight line; there were more detours, false starts, and wrong turns than I can count. But winding as the path may have been, that's still a lot of change for the better in a short amount of time, despite not having any of the advantages that you might expect I would need to make it all happen; no academic credentials (I'm actually a high-school dropout, which is a story for another time), no experience in online marketing (which was new to me at the start of this journey), and no financial resources (being not only broke, but also a quarter of a million dollars in the hole). These things all made me an unlikely character for the protagonist in this sort of a rags-to-riches story, and the fact that I did it (and now teach thousands of others to do the same) is less a testament to me or my abilities, than to the environment and circumstances that made it all possible.

That environment and circumstances created the Teach and Grow Rich opportunity, that I wrote this book to share with you. If you want more of my personal story, you'll find it in an appendix at the end; other than that, I've mostly avoided using myself as an example, because I don't want anyone to think that this book is about me. Rather, it is about the opportunity itself, and I've done my best to illustrate that through as many different examples as I could fit into these pages. But this book isn't about those examples either. My strong conviction is that the best stories of Teach and Grow Rich success have yet to be told, and my hope is that one of the greatest will be yours.

∞ ∞ ∞

This book took an unusual path from idea-in-mind to pages-in-hand. Usually an idea becomes a book proposal, that eventually leads to a deal with a publisher. Drafts are written, edited, and revised, and if all goes well, a book appears on the shelves 12-18 months later.

That isn't what happened with this book. The gestation

period was much longer, and the path from author's brain to reader's hand was lightning fast. The ideas themselves gelled for me over the course of the several years that I spent building and selling courses (for the whole story, see the appendix at the end of this book). Once the big idea had crystallized, though, it was a matter of months before the first edition was published in September of 2015.

That first edition was a manifesto; an introduction to the world of an idea that I had seen first-hand and knew to have merit, based on dozens of case studies that I had observed. It was meant to be an eye-opening think-piece, but not a how-to manual – partially because what excited me was the idea of stretching the minds and horizons of my readers, and partially because I simply didn't have the experience then to lay down a step-by-step process that most readers could use without a lot of support.

In the words of Ralph Waldo Emerson, "the mind, once stretched by a new idea, never returns to its original dimensions". I've been honored and gratified to see that this has been the case for many of the readers of the first edition. I've witnessed this in the incredible success that so many have experienced (some of which I've documented here), in the widespread recognition that building online courses can be a meaningful path to impact and income. The appendix which shares our State of Online Courses industry report demonstrates how perceptions have evolved between then and now, and our entire industry's transition away from the paradigm of information that I called out, and towards the paradigm of education that I preached (though there's still a long, long way to go).

Despite the success of the first edition, not everyone loved it. The biggest complaint against it was the absence of how-to information. I've fixed that in this second edition, both because so many asked for it, and because, finally, I can. Since writing the first edition, I've helped literally thousands of aspiring online educators seize the Teach and Grow Rich opportunity by launching their pilots and courses. This has given me an understanding of the details and nuances of the process that I simply didn't have when I wrote the first edition, and it's a big part of why I've revised the book so extensively - not only updating every section, but also expanding the book to nearly triple its original length.

Remember, though, that even with so much added, there's a limit to what a book can do for you. Yes, I'll share as much as I can in the pages that follow; in Part 1 you'll learn what the Teach and Grow Rich opportunity is and why it is so special, where and when it emerged in Parts 2 and 3, who can seize it in Part 4, and what steps you need to take to do so in Part 5. All along the way, I'll do my best to keep you engrossed and entertained. But a central premise driving these ideas is that information (in all its forms, including this book) is an agent of inspiration, but not transformation. So while I can confidently promise to stretch your mind, expand your horizons, and paint a clear path for you to follow, I can't walk it with you through the pages of a book. Transformation requires ongoing action through the partnership of real education, and that's why I've created a host of additional materials to support you later on the journey that begins here.

Turn the page, then, and let's take the first step together...

5-Minute Whiteboard Video Summary of Teach and Grow Rich

Do you love those short hand-drawn video summaries of the most important and impactful ideas in books? Then you'll love this quick summary of Teach and Grow Rich:

Go here to get the video (and other bonuses), for free:

http://mrse.co/whiteboard

Part 1:
One of These Things
Is Not Like the Others

"Never doubt that a small group of thoughtful, committed people can change the world; indeed, it's the only thing that ever has."

-Margaret Mead

Diane Holmes was a programmer whose career was cut short by chronic illness.

Medical expenses plus the inability to earn meaningful income led to severe financial hardship, and by the summer of 2015 she was forced to sell her car, and was making plans to sell her dining room furniture to make ends meet.

Seemingly grasping at straws, Diane fell back on her passion for fiction writing, which she had taught for the past 25 years. It had never been very lucrative, but faced with the prospect of living in poverty, unable to even afford the prescriptions that she needed to stay well, it was all she had. She decided to teach an online course about a very specific skill of fiction writers: the art of pacing.

Without an ad budget or audience with which to share her course, she thought she'd be lucky to find even a couple of students... which is why she was shocked to enroll 15 paying students in the first four hours, and another 15 by the time she closed enrollment the next day. And that was just the beginning for her Genius Pacing Academy...

∞ ∞ ∞

Lindsey Stirling was 23 when she got her first big break on season five of *America's Got Talent*.

Described as a "hip hop violinist," she had a vision of blending her music with dance. Her performance in the qualifying rounds was well received by the audience, and dubbed "electrifying" by the judges. Then, in her quarterfinal performance, she stepped up the level of dance, and was promptly eliminated from the competition. So much for her big break. In the words of judge Piers Morgan, "you're not untalented, but you're not good enough to get away with flying through the air and trying to play the violin at the same time."

That might have been the end of the story, had cinematographer Devin Graham not contacted her about making a YouTube video for one of her songs. That video was hugely successful, leading to more videos, and greater renown. Her success on YouTube led to being signed by Lady Gaga's manager, two successful albums, and a world tour.

As of this writing, Lindsey's YouTube channel has over a billion and a half total views and over eight and a half million subscribers. Not bad for a woman who just celebrated her thirtieth birthday!

∞ ∞ ∞

Niklas Hed, Jarno Väkenväinen, and Kim Dikert were all

18

students together at the Helsinki University of Technology in 2003.

They joined forces to participate in a mobile game development competition, and won with a real-time multiplayer game called King of the Cabbage World. Emboldened by their success, they set up shop as a game development company called Relude and started cranking out a combination of work-for-hire projects, published games, and independently released titles.

Fast forward six years: they had changed their name to Rovio and released their 52nd game, in which players use a slingshot to launch birds at pigs in or around various structures. It was a runaway success, reaching the number 1 spot on the paid section of the Apple App Store six months later, leading to over a billion downloads in less than two years.

That game was called Angry Birds, and it has spawned a plethora of spin-offs and branded merchandise, and grown Rovio to hundreds of employees and hundreds of millions in annual revenues. Pretty impressive for something that was started by three friends in college!

∞ ∞ ∞

Brian Creager was living a double life; corporate executive by day, and packaged goods manufacturer by... well, earlier in the day.

For more than a year, Brian got up at 3am to start working

on his side hustle before heading off to his day job. That side hustle was selling premium shampoo under his boutique label krieger + söhne. His strategy was to sell to barbers in local markets, and it wasn't going nearly as well as he had initially planned.

Then, in a chance conversation, it was suggested to Brian that he list his shampoo on Amazon. He did, and after seeing some initial success, decided to double-down on the platform. He moved his inventory into Amazon's warehouses (to be picked, packed, and shipped through their "fulfilled by Amazon" program), and immersed himself in the study of Amazon's algorithms – and the more he did, the faster his business grew.

A mere 18 months after starting his business, it had grown to generate revenue that dwarfed his corporate salary.

A Different Kind of Opportunity

These days, you can't throw a stone without hitting someone whose fortune was changed by the power of the internet. The four stories that you just read are instances of that phenomenon. These stories are interesting, and even inspiring... but far from unique. There are thousands of performers who were catapulted to stardom by YouTube, droves of mobile gaming companies that have seen great success in the app market, more product lines and categories than you can count successfully leveraging the fulfillment and distribution of Amazon, and a fast-growing number of independent course creators generating a meaningful income through the impact of their burgeoning education empires.

Whether it's the story of performer Lindsey Sterling, game developer Rovio, Brian Creager's krieger + söhne brand of shampoo and Diane Holmes' Genius Pacing Academy, changing market conditions created new opportunities that they, and many like them, were able to capitalize on. Some were truly prescient in seeing the opportunity before others did, and others were just lucky, in the right place at the right time. Many more were a little later to the party, but still managed to get in while the opportunity was hot.

Despite the commonalities between these inspiring stories, one stands out in several subtle but important ways: Diane Holmes, who turned her life around with the runaway success that was her Genius Pacing Academy course for fiction writers. What sets Diane's story apart is what this book is all about: The Teach and Grow Rich opportunity to create education products that empower others to do what you already know how to do. This opportunity is more exciting than YouTube, mobile games, and Amazon put together, because it is qualitatively different in three important ways: democratized access, the fat tail, and the potential for impact.

Democratized Access: Why Moore's Law Isn't Enough

In 1965, Intel co-founder Gordon Moore observed that the number of transistors per square inch on integrated circuits had doubled every year since their invention. This became codified as Moore's Law, which accurately predicted the exponentially growing power and shrinking cost of computer technology over the past several decades. This was expected to be the ultimate leveler of the playing field, and in many ways, it has been.

Not so long ago, the ability to produce and publish a music video was limited to record labels. But now, Lindsey Stirling and Devin Graham could do it themselves, and publish it to YouTube. Mobile games didn't even exist even a decade before the founders of Rovio were students together in 2003. And krieger + söhne's success completely depended on the rise of e-commerce giant Amazon.

The playing field has been leveled, at least in terms of access to the enabling tools and technologies. But in truth, this sort of success is still largely inaccessible to most people, simply because each of these opportunities requires a very specific set of skills, expertise, or resources that most people just don't have. Becoming a YouTube celebrity takes more than video production technology – you need musical talent, which most of us don't have; the technology of mobile gaming is accessible to everyone, but you still need to know how to write code, which most of us don't. And while anyone can register as a seller with Amazon, you still need a product to sell, and the financial resources to source, stock, and deliver inventory... which most of us can't afford to invest. The same is true for most other "flavor of the month" online opportunities, whether they involve optimizing for Google's coveted search results, running ads on Facebook to various sorts of funnels, leveraging the explosion of visual activity on Instagram, or whatever else – in all cases, even if the basic technologies are accessible to all, capitalizing on them still takes a set of skills or resources that most people don't have.

The Teach and Grow Rich opportunity is different. Yes, you need specialized knowledge about a topic to create a course about it, but your course can be about anything at all. And who among us doesn't have meaningful knowledge about any topic at all? Not only that, the best education products are about a hyper-narrow topic, which means that the list of opportunities is practically endless. In fact, to illustrate just how diverse and narrowly specific successful courses can be, here are a few examples of the topics of courses that I've recently seen succeed (in addition to Diane Holmes's course about pacing for fiction writing):

- how to massage your elderly dog

- how to interpret your dreams

- how to get ahead in your career as a project manager

- how to help children overcome sensory integration challenges

- how to use Evernote to get organized

- how to write a fiction book that people will buy

- how to teach your children math

- how to accelerate the success of a health or wellness practice

These courses are successfully being taught as you read these words, along with hundreds of others (for more examples, see the Gallery of Unlikely Educators appendix at the end of this book). Many of these courses were developed by people who had never taught an online course before. Some started out with impressive credentials, and others had only ever seen their topic as a hobby. Unlike fields that require extensive and formalized training and credentials (think medicine, or law), the expertise that it takes to succeed in producing online courses in most areas tends to be much lower; if you know more than your students, and you know it well enough to teach, this opportunity is wide open to you.

This means that seizing the Teach and Grow Rich isn't just for a small or specialized segment of our society. For once, the playing field is truly level. The winners will be ordinary people who've gained some useful knowledge and skill over their lifetime, and want to make the world around them a little bit better by sharing it with others.

The Short Head vs. The Fat Tail: So 1,000 True Fans Is Enough

The "long tail" is an idea that was popularized by Chris Anderson in his book by the same name. It's a simple concept, with very powerful implications. Here it is in a nutshell, as articulated by Anderson on his website:

> *"...our culture and economy is increasingly shifting away from a focus on a relatively small number of "hits" (mainstream products and markets) at the head of the demand curve and*

toward a huge number of niches in the tail. As the costs of production and distribution fall, especially online, there is now less need to lump products and consumers into one-size-fits-all containers. In an era without the constraints of physical shelf space and other bottlenecks of distribution, narrowly-targeted goods and services can be as economically attractive as mainstream fare."

In other words, shelf space in stores was a limited commodity; there used to be only so much room, so they only stocked the stuff that they knew a lot of people were going to buy (i.e. the "hits"). When things went digital and the concept of shelf space became meaningless, it let all the "non-hits" into the market for those who wanted them. This is fantastic for all those of us whose tastes don't conform to top 40 lists in every category!

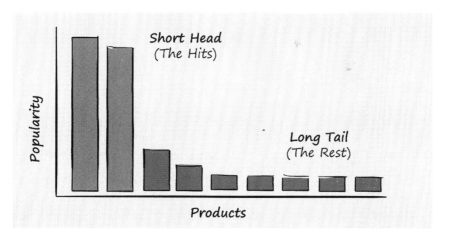

But a product, song, or video that starts in the long tail doesn't always stay there. YouTube allows every musician in the world to post a video for free, even if they don't get a single person to view it (i.e. the very end of the long tail).

But if someone does watch the video, they might share it with their friends. If their friends like it, they might share it as well. If that happens enough times, we say that the video has "gone viral". Essentially, it has climbed the long tail and made it to the short head. That's exactly what happened to Lindsey Stirling on YouTube, Rovio on the App Store (they lived in the long tail for six years before Angry Birds shot to the top of the charts), and krieger + söhne on Amazon.

This is great for the few that make it big with a hit, but what happens to everyone else? In aggregate, their results are spectacular; in fact, sites like Amazon and iTunes see a substantial portion of their traffic and revenue come from the long tail of titles that most of us have never even heard of. But this only works because of the immense quantity of those titles; for the artists and producers who live in the long tail, the returns are dismal. Everybody knows about the hits, but hardly anyone has even heard of the rest. This is true of YouTube video producers (a full third of videos published on YouTube have fewer than 10 views), app developers (94% of the revenue in the Apple App Store comes from just 1% of all publishers, and 60% of apps go un-downloaded), authors on Kindle (the vast majority sell less than a hundred books), and so on, and so forth.

Kevin Kelly's famous concept of "1,000 True Fans" sometimes comes up in defense of the long tail. First published as an article in 1998, the basic idea is that all an artist needs to succeed are 1,000 true fans. With just 1,000 people paying you as little as $100 per year, you can do quite well for yourself. And even if you add as little as 1 true fan a day, you'll reach your target of 1,000 in just under three years. The trouble is that, even if you could get 1,000 people to consume whatever you create (which is easier said than done!), nobody on YouTube, Amazon, or any app store earns anywhere near $100 per sale! These platforms rely on volume to succeed, so they tend to force pricing models that are great for the hits, but not for everyone else. That's why success with most opportunities that rely on long tail economics require that you move large quantities of inventory on a monthly, weekly, or even daily basis.

That works great if you're a Goliath, as Lindsey Stirling, Rovio, and krieger + söhne have all become. But what if you're David, like the majority of participants in any market? In that case, you'd be much better served by selling something of premium value, so you don't need the same volume of sales to turn a meaningful profit. This same long tail versus fat tail economic model plays out on the global scale when you compare China and Germany.

Consider China as the undisputed Goliath of exporting goods to the rest of the world, with a population just under 1.4 billion, and yearly exports of 2.28 trillion dollars in 2015, as reported by the World Bank. Compared to China, Germany is David, with a population of only 81 million. But despite being dwarfed by seventeen-times-larger China, Germany's global exports add up to 1.33 trillion. In other words, Germany's per capita exports are more than ten times China's – because China's typical export is a dollar store doo-dad, and Germany's typical export is a luxury sedan.

The Teach and Grow Rich opportunity is different from most opportunities that are governed by long tail economics because education commands a premium price. And when you're able to charge a premium, you don't need enormous volume to do very well. Consider Diane Holmes's Genius Pacing Academy. She enrolled 30 students in her pilot course; an order of magnitude more than she expected, but a far cry from Lindsey Stirling's eight and a half million YouTube subscribers or Rovio's billion app downloads! And yet, 30 students were enough to form a lucrative base for Diane to build on, and her Genius Pacing Academy has gone on to generate a comfortable income for her. The profitability math works with the Teach and Grow Rich opportunity for two reasons:

1. These courses are typically sold directly by their creators. This means that they aren't constrained by the pricing drivers of long tail platforms like iTunes or Amazon, nor do they have to pay sizeable cuts to middlemen. And while individual course creators don't have the reach or distribution of a platform like Amazon or iTunes, they can reach more than enough students to do very well for themselves.

2. Whereas our modern context has led us to expect videos, apps, and even e-books to be cheap or free, we're accustomed to paying a premium for real education, because we know that it's worth it. Unlike mere information, education promises a transformation of our knowledge or abilities that is worth paying for – as we'll explore in much greater detail in the next chapter.

For both of these reasons, education products such as courses can (and do!) sell for prices in the range of $50 to $5,000, and often with the course creator keeping a larger portion of that price than most other platforms would allow. And so long as those courses deliver on their promises, they're seen as bargains by the students whose lives they transform. So instead of the usual long tail distribution of success, the Teach and Grow Rich opportunity will follow a fat tail distribution; relatively fewer big hits, and a lot more moderate successes.

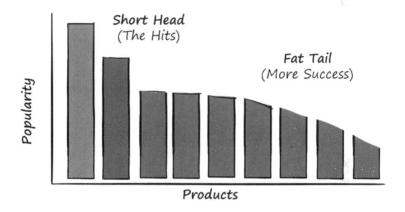

With a few notable exceptions (like Lynda.com, which was acquired by LinkedIn in April of 2015 for a billion and a half dollars), the hits won't make billions, and the long tail won't be left with peanuts. Instead, there will be a fat tail of successes earning $50K, $200K, or $1M at a time. Diane Holmes is one example, and there are many others whose stories you'll encounter later in this book.

This is bad news for venture investors in Silicon Valley, because it means there won't be many of the hundred million- or billion-dollar successes that they need to bet on. But for most people, who want to create a better life for themselves, their families, and the world around them, this just might be the most exciting opportunity that's come around in a very long time. Most especially because there's more than just money to be made here...

Value vs. Impact:
Making Money by Helping Others

At the tender age of 12, Ray Dalio bought a few shares in Northeast Airlines, and his investment promptly tripled in value when the airline merged with another company. That was just the beginning; Dalio eventually founded Bridgewater Associates, which grew to become the largest hedge fund in the world, with over $160 billion in assets under management. He predicted the global financial crisis of 2008 before it happened, and has since published a number of essays and videos providing free high-level financial education to the public.

One topic that Dalio de-mystifies is the concept of debt, which is a key driver of the modern economy. He explains that, despite popular misconceptions, debt isn't always a bad thing. In fact, debt can be a powerful engine for economic empowerment and growth. The key is to distinguish between "good debt" and "bad debt". Put simply, good debt is money borrowed for investment in things that will improve your financial wellbeing, like real-estate and education. With those investments, you either have an asset that will appreciate, or an increased ability to earn, or both. If you're careful not to take on more than you can afford to eventually repay, good debt can be the key to growing your skill-set and earning power. Bad debt, on the other hand, is money borrowed to buy things that won't create a financial return, like a new television and gaming console. Once that money is spent, it's gone forever. Strategically assuming good debt while diligently minimizing or avoiding bad debt is a big part of the recipe for financial successes like Dalio's.

But if you look more closely, it's about more than just maximizing our financial net worths. After all, money isn't the end goal – it's just the means for creating the lifestyle, experiences, and impact that we care about. So while scrutinizing and evaluating debt is a critical skill in our modern economy (both because so many of us have so much of it, and because the carrying costs can be crippling), the "good" versus "bad" analysis doesn't just apply to things we buy with borrowed money. In fact, every transaction will either make our lives better ("good"), worse ("bad"), or just maintain the status quo.

Most of our spending is in that third category; maintaining our lifestyles and keeping us at the level of happiness and capability that we're already at. Think groceries, clothing, entertainment, etc. – if paid for with debt, these are "bad" transactions, because it means living unsustainably, beyond our means. If we can afford them, though, these transactions are neutral; their lack can make us miserable, but their presence isn't enough for us to thrive.

Some of our spending goes towards things that we might want in the moment, even though we know that they're bad for us. Think junk food, alcohol, tobacco, or gambling; okay to indulge in from time to time, but with deleterious effects on our lives if taken to excess. Whether we can afford them or not, these are not good places to invest our resources.

For most of us, only a small portion of our money and energy is truly dedicated to things that make us better, smarter, happier, and more capable by expanding our minds and horizons. And this is the real beauty and magic of the Teach and Grow Rich opportunity that this book is all about. There are lots of ways to make money by creating something that others will be happy to pay you for. But only in a few of those cases will you grow rich by genuinely improving the lives of your customers, by empowering them to know more, do better, and be more capable of facing the challenges in their own lives. That's what makes this opportunity so resonant to so many: at the end of the day, most of us care about leaving our world a little better than we found it. Which brings us back to a very important question: what does it mean to grow "rich," anyway?

Teach and Grow... Rich?

If you teach, you will grow rich – that is the bold promise made in the title of this book. I chose it because it paints a clear and accurate picture of what I have to offer, so long as you follow the strategic framework that I'll share in the rest of these pages... and also as a respectful nod to Napoleon

Hill. But despite its accuracy, this title runs the risk of being lumped in with hucksters who promise an effort-free ticket to internet millionairedom, driving fancy cars in circles around supermodels gathered on your private island – and that is emphatically NOT what I have (or care) to offer!

Now, don't get me wrong. Money is important, especially if you don't have enough of it. I know that first-hand, having climbed out of the quarter-of-a-million-dollar hole that I landed in following the implosion my start-up company in 2007. There's no question that being able to comfortably provide for your loved ones is infinitely better than scrounging to make ends meet. I'm grateful for that financial freedom, as are many of the case studies and examples profiled in this book – and if you're in a position where finances are still a struggle, then of course the richness that you seek to grow into includes money.

After achieving a level of financial success, though, most realize that while the absence of money can make you miserable, having a lot won't make you happy. As Abraham Maslow's Hierarchy of Needs teaches us, once our basic needs are provided for, we need more to live a truly rich life: we need freedom, and the opportunity for impact. Freedom comes in different shades and hues, like...

The freedom to choose your own hours. That can mean working mornings, nights, weekdays, weekends, or whatever schedule works for you, your temperament, your family, and your priorities.

The freedom to travel. That can mean taking that dream vacation that you've been waiting for, going on extended trips, or living the life of a digital nomad – as everything you'll learn in this book can be done from anywhere you can find a reliable internet connection.

The freedom to do stuff that matters. That can mean focusing your work around the causes and transformations that you care about, or having the resources and free time to dedicate to the hobbies and causes that are most important to you.

Which brings us to impact. Work for so many is unfortunate drudgery, taking us away from the people and causes that we care about. The Teach and Grow Rich opportunity reverses that pattern, by connecting us to the people that we care most about serving, and doing work that makes the greatest possible difference to others – both individually, and as a society.

It all starts with a single student. We've all had our lives touched by a great teacher who saw in us something that we didn't even see in ourselves yet, and gave us the knowledge, skills, and confidence to become that best version of who we are. That's the role that the Teach and Grow Rich opportunity invites us to play, and while that work is rewarding to the teacher, the real winner is the student. Take that impact and transformation, and multiply it by a thousand students, and the effect is tremendous. Consider the ripple effects, and you single-handedly nudge the world in a slightly better direction.

What better way is there to make a rich, generous living than by enriching the lives of others? What dedication of our time and energy would we feel more proud to tell our parents and children about? That drive to contribute and make a difference is what characterizes the entrepreneurs that I have the privilege of working with, and that is what the Teach and Grow Rich opportunity makes possible: leveraging what you know to empower others, and make the world a better place in the ways that matter to you the most.

In Summary (TL;DR)

For over a decade, the Internet slang expression "TL;DR" (short for "too long; didn't read") has been used by conscientious communicators to share a brief summary of a longer passage; so, for example, if I forwarded you a seven page article, I'd add in my email a note saying "tl;dr – the key point being made here is [whatever the key point is]".

Now, I sincerely hope that the writing and content of this book merits a full and detailed reading, but just in case you're skimming or want to review later, each chapter will end with a brief "TL;DR" summary. Here are some of the key points that we covered in this chapter:

- The power of the internet and changing market conditions have changed the fortunes of people like fiction writing educator Diane Holmes, hip hop violinist Lindsey Stirling, game developers Niklas Hed, Jarno Väkenväinen, and Kim Dikert, and premium shampoo vendor Brian Creager.

- The Teach and Grow Rich opportunity stands out in three important ways: democratized access, the fat tail, and potential for impact.

- **Democratized Access:** Other opportunities require a very specific set of skills, expertise, and resources most people don't have. On the other hand, the opportunity to create education products exists for anyone who knows more than their students do and knows it well enough to teach others.

- **The Fat Tail:** The Teach and Grow Rich opportunity doesn't follow the long tail distribution that characterizes most markets, where the few who go viral make most of the earnings, while everyone else has dismal returns. An online course can be about almost anything at all. And since people are accustomed to paying a premium for real education, course creators don't need to rely on volume to succeed. This means the field is open for more people to have great successes.

- **Potential for Impact:** Online creators can create value and make an impact by empowering others to know more, do more, and better face their challenges.

- If you teach, you will grow rich, and this is about more than just financial freedom. It also means having the freedom to shape your own lifestyle, do work that's meaningful, and make the world a better place.

Now that we've recapped, let's move on to the next chapter and see where this opportunity came from in the first place...

Case in Point:
Amber Copeland's Mind-Body Ballroom

To help make the ideas in each part of this book feel more "real," I've sprinkled these "Case in Point" sections sharing illustrative case studies throughout these pages. Each is meant to illustrate the concepts described in the preceding section, and I've intentionally avoided the "look how they made millions overnight" variety that happen, but aren't representative or attainable for most. These results are realistic, practical, and illustrative of what most people applying these ideas are likely to experience.

Our first of these case studies is Amber Copeland, a ballroom dancer and instructor who is a great example of the Teach and Grow Rich opportunity in action.

Illness prevented Amber from continuing to give as many face-to-face classes as she used to, and she found her income dwindling. Normally, this would have ended her career in ballroom dancing. In fact, Amber feared she would have to give up teaching altogether.

And so she began to look for ways to teach others online through video programs. She wasn't familiar with the technology involved. Neither was she knowledgeable of the sales process required for her to sell her programs.

But online course creation offers democratized access. Almost anybody can be an online course creator—including Amber, who didn't have an audience, internet savvy, or a big marketing budget. Armed with a desire to share her passion with other ballroom dancers, Amber launched her first online course.

She sent a survey to everyone she knew in the ballroom dancing industry, including her clients and peers. By asking one simple question, she learned their biggest challenge in ballroom dance. That helped her figure out what topic to build her pilot course around.

Although she had a very small online following, she was able to present her pilot course offer to 60 people. Her goal was to sell five spots for $197 each, and she reached that target within one week. This illustrates the fat tail of online course creation. Amber didn't need thousands or even hundreds of students to earn a moderate income. She found people who were willing to pay more than the cost of, say, a ballroom dancing DVD in exchange for the personalized support she could provide.

Amber, despite her limited prominence and online presence, charges more for her online course than Julianne Hough does for her ballroom dancing DVD ($6.19 on Amazon.com).

Finally, Amber's story shows how online course creators can create value and impact. Through online courses, Amber continues to do what she loves—teaching body awareness for ballroom competitive dancers—and support herself despite her illness.

In fact, Amber can make an even greater impact now with

online courses than she did with in-person classes when she was healthy. Whereas previously, Amber was teaching one-to-one, now she can reach one-to-many.

There are many like Amber, who struggle with life changes and other situations that threaten their livelihood. They need to reach more people and make a bigger impact without having to work themselves to the bone. For some of them, the Teach and Grow Rich opportunity is the key to building a business around the lifestyle that works for them, while delivering value to those they teach.

Part 2:
When Worlds Collide

"The secret of change is to focus all of your energy, not on fighting the old, but on building the new."

- Socrates

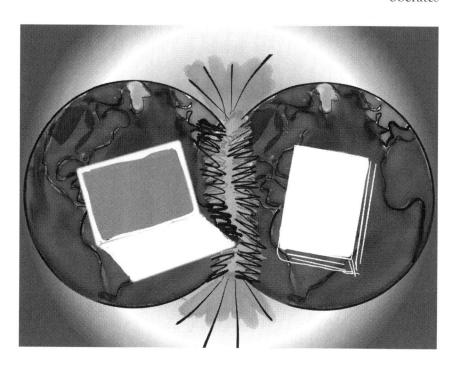

If you take too much in life for granted, the "easy" solution might be to have a child (or borrow one for a few weeks). A child can bring a new appreciation for the simplest things, like being able to sleep past 6am, walk barefoot to the kitchen without stepping on Legos, or not have to explain why climbing into the dishwasher isn't an exciting new game. If you don't have kids, I'll bet none of these ever crossed your mind, and if you do then you know exactly what I mean!

Having kids also teaches you not to take for granted the unwritten rules that govern our lives. Water is allowed in bed, but not juice. You can eat pasta with your hands, but not yogurt. You can play with Mommy's phone, but not Daddy's. And sometimes, different worlds with different unwritten rules collide – which will win? You're allowed to play with Mommy's phone, but aren't allowed to play with phones at Grandma's house – so can you play with Mommy's phone at Grandma's house? Watching children sort out the unwritten rules of the world around them helps us all remember how contrived, arbitrary and context-specific these rules can be.

If you don't have kids, think of two television shows that deal in the same setting and subject matter, but with very different unwritten rules; *House MD* versus *Scrubs*, *The West Wing* versus *House of Cards*, or *The Wire* versus *Brooklyn Nine-Nine*. Then try to imagine what would happen if those two worlds met. How would *The West Wing*'s wise and upstanding President Jed Bartlett fare in the seedy and scheming political landscape of Frank Underwood's *House of Cards*? How would the acerbic and defiant Gregory House fare at the light and comical Sacred Heart Hospital of *Scrubs*... would he be the undisputed ruler of the roost, or would he be fired on his first day? It's hard to guess because it's not just the characters that are different – it's the unwritten rules of the entire world that they live in, and when those rules collide, it can be challenging to predict what will happen.

This is just a thought exercise when it comes to phone privileges at Grandma's house, or the interactions of fictional characters in make believe worlds. But when worlds collide in real life, the stakes can be very, very high (case in point: Donald Trump was the unlikely candidate in the 2016 presidential election precisely because he came from a world outside the political landscape, with a very different set of unwritten rules... and to the surprise of many, he won the presidency over political veteran Hillary Clinton). And it's just such a collision of worlds – the glacially slow-moving world of education, and the lightning-paced world of online business – that is driving the Teach and Grow Rich opportunity.

Education:
Where It Was, and Where It's Going

The late 1970s and early 1980s were the heyday of modern higher education. Technology and globalization had made businesses bigger and more complex, and entering the job market called for higher levels of knowledge, skill and training. Not only that, thriving in the work force also required an academic foundation that allowed for both adaptability and continued professional development over the course of a career. Jobs requiring just a high school education were beginning to disappear, but lifelong employment was still very much a reality, so higher education was legitimately the ticket to a life of prosperity.

You got that education at an institution of higher learning, and if you were very lucky, at a top school like Harvard, Yale, or Stanford. It wasn't cheap, and would take several years to complete, but it was more than worth the investment and corresponding student loan debt. You'd emerge into the job market with a degree that distinguished you from aspiring applicants, and qualified you for employment that would pay for the cost of the degree many times over during the life of your career.

But that was many decades ago, and a lot has changed since then. Higher education is no longer a surefire ticket to a good job; depending on the sources you read, underemployment for university graduates is anywhere from 16% to 44%. To understand why this is the case, we must first understand why degrees were ever a path to prosperity in the first place

– and it's not for the reason that most people think.

At the core, a university degree was only ever important as a shortcut for assessing what it's bearer brings to the table. In some cases, like a legal, medical, or accounting designation, it's a confirmation of technical skills that are crucial to the performance of certain kinds of work. But with many arts and business degrees, the degree really only tells a prospective employer two important things: that you were smart enough to get into college (i.e. college admissions has already screened you, and found you worthy), and that you have enough of a work ethic to complete a 4-year program. Now, if a hiring manager looking to fill a position sees twenty resumes and only two have earned a university degree, they easily float to the top of the pile. And in the late 1970s and early 1980s, that was exactly the case; a university education was rare enough to be a meaningful differentiator in the eyes of a prospective employer. It was the golden ticket, and its price over the past several decades has skyrocketed.

But the days of a university education as golden ticket have passed. Today, these degrees have become nearly ubiquitous among the seekers of good jobs. Not only that, but employers are also starting to realize that other than the general filtering of knowing that a candidate was good enough to get into college, the university experience doesn't actually qualify them to do much of anything. Hence the underemployment figures that I just mentioned, and the record numbers of adult children returning home to live with their parents after completing their educations.

The value of higher education has been declining for some time now, but it's been so iconic as a golden ticket for so long, that change comes slowly. After all, young people considering whether to pursue higher education or some other path take their cues from people who are far enough along in their lives and careers to be able to look back and say what worked and what didn't – except that those far enough along grew up in a different time, when a general university education conveyed a far more advantages than it currently does. Some millennials are already speaking out about the lack of benefits and mountain of debt that they were saddled with by their education, but general awareness of this shift is still a few years away. So the cost of a university education continues to rise, as it has by an order of magnitude over the past few decades (faster than the stock market and inflation combined). Most people don't have that kind of money, so they turn to student loans, and every year more students graduate with hundreds of thousands of dollars in debt, and no prospects for meaningful employment.

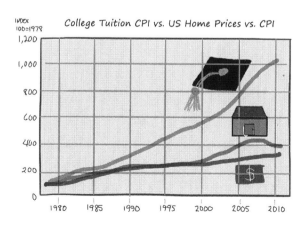

College Tuition CPI vs. US Home Prices vs. CPI

Clearly, this state of affairs isn't sustainable, and many

eyebrows are already being raised at the value of a university degree. The sentiment was articulated well by Kansas State University student Billy Willson, who completed his first semester with a grade point average of 4.0, and promptly dropped out, calling the entire experience a scam. Here is an excerpt of the public notice that he posted on Facebook about his decision (full statement and more details at http://www.anonews.co/college-student-scammed/):

> "You are being put thousands into debt to learn things you will never even use. Wasting 4 years of your life to be stuck at a paycheck that grows slower than the rate of inflation. Paying $200 for a $6 textbook. Being taught by teachers who have never done what they're teaching. Average income has increased 5x over the last 40 years while cost of college has increased 18x."

Now, don't get me wrong; education is still critically important to our society, and higher education has an important role to play. Vocational training for professions like medicine, law, accounting, and engineering will always be needed, as will advanced training in technical fields like math and sciences. But the general arts or business degree that "teaches you how to think" has outlived its mainstream value, and we can look forward to a massive contraction of the education industrial complex over the coming decades (one of the first to have already fallen is the public company ITT Educational Services Inc., which abruptly shut down over 130 campuses and left 40,000 students stranded in late 2016). The Ivy league and other top-tier schools will do just fine, but mid-tier schools that charge an arm and a leg while delivering little in return are headed for history's dustbin.

People will continue to need and want education, of course, but that desire is growing fragmented; less of "I want a degree that teaches me lots of theory on a topic", and more of "I want a course that teaches me how to accomplish a specific objective". The infrastructure of higher education just isn't equipped to provide that sort of education for a variety of reasons:

It's not what or how professors know how to teach. They're qualified, trained, and accustomed to teaching particular topics in particular ways, many of which aren't compatible with what the market is looking for today. And many of them have tenure, so it'll be a generation before any major progress is likely to happen in this area.

Accreditation functions as golden handcuffs. They protect consumers by enforcing standards, but those standards are slow to evolve, and so institutions can only evolve their curricula so far while remaining accredited.

The economic incentives aren't aligned for change. As overpriced as it might seem to pay thousands upon thousands of dollars for a single course, that's nothing compared to the hundreds of thousands of dollars that students pay for an entire degree. If you ran the school, would you want students to start buying courses at a tiny fraction of the price?

The bottom line is simple: whatever you think of traditional education, the cost has never been higher and the prospects of graduates have never been worse. And yet, we live in a world where learning and education are critical and highly valued on both personal and professional levels. So if the market wants more and better education, and traditional suppliers of education aren't able to deliver, where will we go to get the education that we need in the days ahead?

The answer to that question is emerging in the unlikeliest of places, because the staid and outdated education industry is just beginning to collide with the vigor and energy of independent online education entrepreneurs...

A Short History of "Making Money Online"

In January of 1848, James W. Marshall found gold in Coloma, California. The news quickly spread, and over the following years hundreds of thousands of people flocked to California from across the United States and abroad. At first, the gold was so plentiful that nuggets could be picked up off the ground. When that was gone, the gold seekers had to grow more sophisticated with techniques – like panning and mining. Right around that time, a few entrepreneurs hit upon a realization that would make them richer than most of the gold seekers: There was much easier money to be made selling shovels than actually digging for gold!

The story of online content entrepreneurship follows a similar trajectory. It began less than 20 years ago (Google was founded in 1998, just to put things in context). Back then it wasn't about online education at all; it was just about publishing primarily text based content, like articles. Many of the very early successes happened half by accident; someone with a bit of technical ability would create a website about something they felt passionate about, and one morning they'd wake up and realize that their passion project had attracted hundreds of thousands of followers. Remember, this was the early days; if you built a good website on a topic, it was probably the only one, so getting noticed was just a matter of time. Many of these content publishers never set out to do anything more than write about the topic they cared about; amassing an audience was just a happy accident.

But the game changed in 2003, when Google launched their AdSense platform. This new technology allowed publishers to place a snippet of code on their site, have Google ads served up to their readers, and participate in the profits. That's how some of the very first fortunes were made in the world of online publishing, allowing people to supplement their income, and in some cases quit their day jobs. Those accidental entrepreneurs shared their success stories with friends and colleagues, and encouraged them to jump on this exciting new opportunity. Some did, and the ranks of online publishing businesses grew from dozens, to hundreds, and even more.

Now, as inspiring and exciting as this might sound, the truth is that even a few thousand success stories is barely a blip on the radar of a national or global economy. As a reference point, there were 1,810 reported billionaires in the world in 2016; hardly a volume that makes the outcome feel attainable to most! Making your fortune through online publishing wasn't nearly as easy or straight-forward as some presented it to be, but the idea that it was possible captivated the imaginations of a generation of aspiring online entrepreneurs. And right around then, some people reached the same conclusion as those early gold rushers: it might be easier to sell shovels than to dig for gold. This was bound to happen; with that much demand for the blueprint to online riches, sooner or later someone was bound to step in and create an offer to supply it. That is exactly what happened, in the form of the very first e-books and newsletters teaching how to make money online.

For those who were present and tuned in, these were exciting times – but most of the world didn't even know it was going on. Most of the noise and excitement in the press was around dot com startups with millions of dollars in venture capital backing. In comparison, stories about the occasional blogger turned internet millionaire just weren't sexy enough to be worth mentioning. So to most people, what seemed to happen was that on a few rare occasions, someone actually built a successful business online, while tons of marketers tried to sell snake oil about how to get rich on the internet.

So it took a little longer, but eventually the idea that anyone could start a website and build a profitable online business began to enter into mainstream consciousness – with books like Tim Ferriss's *4-Hour Workweek* (published in 2007) adding fuel to the fire. It wasn't just the global reach and minimal startup cost that was so enticing; the most appealing part to many was the idea of a digital product, which meant you could sell something that wouldn't cost a cent to fulfill. It was the pharmaceutical business model (the first pill costs a billion dollars to develop, and the second costs a penny to produce), without the up-front billion dollar costs of research and development.

There was still a missing piece to the puzzle, though: the fat tail economics described earlier in this book. Sure, if you could sell enough copies, you might make a living selling $20 or even $100 e-books... but you were unlikely to do more than replace a decent salaried income. The phenomenon of the independent internet millionaire really came into its own when people shifted away from publishing, and started "teaching" – because even if you attracted a fraction as many customers, there was just a lot more money to be made with $2,000 courses than with $100 e-books. This transition has driven the explosion of opportunity within the cottage industry of online publishing and teaching, culminating in multi-million dollar launches of multi-thousand-dollar information products. Literally hundreds of thousands of people have more than replaced their employment income; the 2014 U.S Census Bureau reported 852,751 "non-employer" firms (government-speak for solo entrepreneurs, many of which are doing business online) making between $250,000-$2,499,999 – and the number has continued to grow.

But it isn't all entrepreneurial unicorns and rosebuds... while the collision of the glacially slow-moving world of education with the lightning-paced world of online entrepreneurship has created incredible opportunities for some, it has also

TEACH AND GROW RICH

created big problems for many others.

Collision:
Where Two Worlds Meet

In the early 1800s, Russian author Ivan Andreevich Krylov wrote *The Inquisitive Man*, a fable about a man who goes to a museum and notices all sorts of tiny objects, but fails to notice a giant elephant. Sixty years later, Fyodor Dostoevsky wrote about a character in one of his novels that "was just like Krylov's Inquisitive Man, who didn't notice the elephant in the museum". Slowly but surely, the idea of "the elephant in the room" worked its way into our collective vocabulary for describing an obvious-seeming truth that goes unaddressed because it is uncomfortable to bring up.

When it comes to the idea and opportunity to make money online, the biggest elephant in the room is that the people making the most money seem to be the ones teaching others how to make money, and that the whole thing seems reminiscent of a pyramid scheme ("buy my product about making money online, so you can make money online by teaching yet more people how to make money online"). Some of that perception is true, and some isn't, but it's all worth examining and getting out in the open, because it is instructive about the nature and maturity of the Teach and Grow Rich opportunity, and the context that makes it possible.

So let's begin by separating fiction from fact. It isn't accurate to say that the only people making money are those teaching others how to make money, but most noteworthy successes do fall into three broad categories: health and fitness, dating and relationships, and making money. And yes, making money is the largest of the three. This isn't because opportunity resides solely in these areas (I've personally seen tens of millions of dollars made in other areas, and know of hundreds of millions more), but rather because these three topic areas are the tip of the spear, and have been throughout the history of commerce. Health, love, and money are the most basic human needs, which means that more of us are so eager (and sometimes desperate) for them that we'll tolerate risks and forgive deficiencies that we wouldn't in other areas of life.

It's the market's over-eagerness that made it possible for the first online publishers to successfully sell what they believed to be education, complete with the exponentially larger price tags that go with it. And to be clear, the early entrepreneurs who started this trend meant well; they wanted to reach and help more people (which is great), and they wanted more free time to spend with their families (which is also great). So they figured, why not "teach" what they know through the internet, in a way that can reach lots of people, without having to be directly implicated in the process? That's where the wave of "information products" started. The problem was that most of these people weren't teachers at all, so they just didn't understand education well enough to know what it takes to do it right!

Information vs. Education:
Learning to Know vs. Learning to Do

My daughter was born on May 11, 2015. She was a breech baby, which means that she was facing the wrong way in the womb (I think she got her mother's sense of direction) – so it was a planned C-section.

We arrived at the hospital, checked in (kind of like you would at a hotel), and they prepped my wife for surgery. They rolled her in, and after 20 minutes or so they let me in to the operating room. She was lying on the table with a drape over her chest so she and I couldn't see the doctor operate.

My job was simple: talk to my wife, and help her stay as calm as possible. So we chit-chatted, talked about impending parenthood, and made jokes. Then she said she felt a pulling sensation, and a moment later we heard our daughter's first cry of protest at being unexpectedly removed from the womb.

They cleaned her up and brought her over to our side of the curtain. The nurse said "Here's your daughter", and handed her to me – without so much as a word of instruction about what to do with her, or even how to hold her.

So there I was, awkwardly holding my tiny daughter, trying to soothe her so she wouldn't cry (we were still in surgery, so I was worried about disturbing the doctor!), introduce her to my wife (which was tricky, given that she was lying on a table surrounded by medical equipment), and keep my wife calm through the rest of the procedure.

It was wonderful, and hectic, and overwhelming. In hindsight, it was the perfect introduction to what it means to be a parent, which is the ultimate "learn by doing" experience.

Now of course, we had bought the baby books, taken the parenting classes, read the articles, watched the YouTube videos, and listened to countless hours of advice from the many people who cared enough to offer it. But being a parent is something that you can't really prepare for. It's just too far out of your existing frame of reference. And on top of that, every baby really is unique, which means the process of learning how to be a parent has to be unique, too – which is why it is one of the only challenges in the world that we expect and allow people to undertake without any meaningful preparatory education, beyond a handful of books and articles.

Now imagine that same hospital room scenario, except that now it's the doctor being handed the surgical tools and a stack of medical textbooks, with the message of "here, figure it out." That would never fly, because we would never trust someone to operate on us (or handle our legal affairs, or design our buildings, or do anything else that matters) without having a proper education in their field – no matter how much information on the topic they may have consumed.

A Chinese proverb tells us that "to know and not to do is really not to know." We don't expect a soon-to-be parent to internalize everything they read in a book or watched in a YouTube video; they may "know", but they don't know enough to actually "do". In other words, they may have a literacy on the topic that grants them a limited degree of understanding, but they lack the fluency that would make it possible to function competently.

The implicit assumption of those online entrepreneurs who set out (with the best of intentions) to digitize and automate the teaching process was that all the costs that go into creating a traditional educational experience (rent, utilities, accreditation, and of course, teachers) are as superfluous to the process of learning as actual paper books are to the process of reading – but they aren't. You can read just as well on a Kindle as you can on paper, but you can't learn just as well from a video as you can from a good teacher. Videos might be enough to get you to the literacy of "knowing", but it usually takes more to get to the fluency of actual competent "doing".

But those accidental online entrepreneurs didn't know that. They rolled out their information products with great success, because a great many people were eager for the outcomes being promised. The vast majority of the people who bought these products achieved very little, which makes perfect sense; it takes a lot more than information to empower someone to do something they don't already know how to do; even if we understand the concepts, that doesn't mean we have the ability to apply them to achieve the outcomes we care about.

But some students did succeed. They were in the right

place at the right time, and combined hard work with just the right mix of motivation, need, and past experience. All the pieces fit into place for them, and they saw incredible successes. They became the case studies and testimonials that gave hope to the next batch of customers – so much hope, because the results were so great, that the next cohort was willing to pay even higher prices. The cycle continued, and continued, and continued, until the industry was filled with drastically overpriced information products that only helped a tiny fraction of the people who bought them. Some argue that this is a matter of poorly designed content, or misaligned incentives, and there's some truth to those positions. But the real issue goes much deeper: at the heart of the matter are two fundamentally different paradigms of business.

The Difference Between a Textbook and a School

Clearly, it isn't sustainable for people to keep investing top dollar in courses and products that don't deliver the outcomes they're looking for. The industry has to change, and to understand what that change must look like, we must understand the difference between two competing paradigms of business that are at war here: publishing on the one side, and education on the other. In a publishing business, the entrepreneur's job is to produce something that customers want to buy, and that's where their responsibility ends. Once someone has bought a book from a bookstore, for example, nobody owes that customer anything – not the publisher, not the author, and not the bookstore owner.

But that's not how it works when you enroll in a school or university. They're educational institutions, not publishers, and that means they have a much greater responsibility to their students. Of course, students have to show up and do the work, but as long as they live up to what's expected of them, all parties expect the institution to do everything they can to support their students, including investment in teachers and support services to ensure that success. That's why university courses cost so much more than books in bookstores; universities have to pay for rent, utilities, accreditation, and, oh yeah – teachers!

This distinction is usually clear and straightforward; we all understand without needing any sort of explanation that buying a copy of *The American Red Cross First Aid and Safety Handbook* doesn't certify you in CPR, and a subscription to *The New England Journal of Medicine* doesn't make you a doctor. You can certainly learn a lot from those resources, but how much you take away from them (as compared with the next person to pick up a copy) is a personal choice for you to make, that no one will hold you accountable for – least of all the publishers!

On the other hand, if you're accepted into a medical school and you choose to invest the money, time, and effort needed to complete your studies, there is an implicit understanding and expectation that, so long as you do your part and live up to their standards and requirements, you will come out the other end with a diploma certifying you as a Medical Doctor. And it isn't about the certification itself, but rather about what it represents. The diploma is a symbol of proof to the outside world, attesting to the outcome of the educational covenant between yourself and the institution where you completed your studies; that you and they will pool your efforts and resources, partnering in the goal of training and empowering you as a medical professional.

That's why you can't just buy a medical degree the way that you might buy a textbook. In the context of education, there are expectations and responsibilities held by both parties; the student is responsible to dedicate the time and energy it takes to do the work, and the educator is responsible to facilitate the goal of learning through some combination of explanation, simulation, and coaching while working with real patients under expert supervision. The tuition doesn't buy you a medical license, it only buys you the opportunity to earn one – and it takes an enormous amount of labor, resources, and expertise to create that learning opportunity, which is why medical school tuition costs orders of magnitude more than the textbooks that contain the same body of information.

Two Paradigms of Business

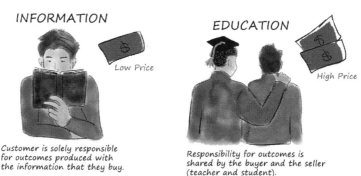

INFORMATION

Low Price

Customer is solely responsible for outcomes produced with the information that they buy.

EDUCATION

High Price

Responsibility for outcomes is shared by the buyer and the seller (teacher and student).

The bottom line is that information and education serve very different purposes, and are governed by very different economics. Information is meant to inform, inspire, and act as a reference. It can generally be created once and then sold many times with little marginal cost, so it is usually cheap. Education, on the other hand, is meant to empower and transform. This generally requires a partnership between student and teacher that involves more hands-on guidance and support, so it usually comes at a premium. Each is valuable in its own right, and complements the other very well.

The problems begin, however, when information is masqueraded as education, and sold at a premium... which is precisely the state of affairs in the world of online content publishing.

Entrepreneurs saw the instant-access and zero-cost fulfillment that made digital content more attractive than print, with no loss in experience and, if anything, an increase in quality (it can be updated more regularly, can contain links to other resources, etc.). They assumed that it would work just as well with education as it did with information, so they did away with the classrooms, the textbooks, and the teachers, to be replaced by membership sites, PDF downloads, and video lessons.

But whereas a Kindle book provides every bit as good a reading experience as a paper copy did, the same isn't true about the process of automating education; take away the learning environments and teachers, and you're left with nothing more than a glorified multi-media textbook. And yet those glorified textbooks are being sold for far, far more than the outcomes they create could ever justify.

Now, to be clear: I have nothing against products costing money, or even costing a lot of money. Honestly, in my experience, it's very rare to become successful without making significant investments in the path you've chosen, because making an investment signals to yourself that you're serious, and most people need help to learn and succeed. Getting that help can and should cost money, and investments in good education are some of the best that we can make. What is completely unsustainable is charging premium prices for information without offering any of the help or support that would be needed to produce results.

Aftershock:
The Market Correcting Itself

This sort of mismatch between what things cost and the value they provide is never sustainable, and people are already realizing that the emperor has no clothes; overpriced information products are getting harder to sell, and customers that buy them are becoming increasingly difficult to retain.

When price and value are misaligned in any market, there are only two things that can happen: either the price will adjust to reflect the value, or the value will adjust to reflect the price. In this particular case, both will happen. The current market for digital products is already splitting into two camps: low-cost information on one side, and premium education on the other.

Those businesses that stick to the publishing model will be forced to drop their prices significantly over the coming years, as the market's willingness to pay these inflated prices completely disappears. This is already happening through marketplaces like Amazon. As one of the world's single biggest retailers, they know better than most what the market is willing to bear, and it only takes a moment of browsing Kindle books to see that digital information tends to be valued in the $1-$20 range.

Now, video content takes more work to produce, so for that we might look at Udemy, which is one of the world's largest course marketplaces (we'll examine several other businesses of this sort in the next chapter). When the first edition of *Teach and Grow Rich* was published in 2015, Udemy course prices varied wildly, from free to as high as $500 or more (though most of their sales were made through steep time-limited discounts). Since then, Udemy has instituted new pricing policies that sharply constrain what price course creators can charge. This is perfectly in line with this chapter's prediction that most information product sellers will see prices drop significantly, and return to the same long tail distribution where the few mega-hits that sell millions of copies rake in the vast majority of the profits.

And will some online publishers continue to charge a premium? Yes, of course – outliers will always exist, but even with the outliers, premium information (which is a bit of an oxymoron) will increasingly come bundled with the things that actually justify those prices, like software, or support… and when you add support to the mix, you start toeing the line that divides information from education.

That's the other direction in which online entrepreneurs can go: embrace the paradigm of education, and take ownership of their responsibility to truly partner with their students in pursuit of the learning goals they care about achieving. Those who follow this route will continue to command premium prices, and they'll do so with increasing ease, as the growing sophistication of the market phases the peddlers of overpriced information out of the picture.

For those who choose to embrace the opportunity to become Educator Entrepreneurs, the next decade looks very bright. Intuitively, most of the online business world already grasps this; before publishing the first edition of this book in 2015, my team conducted an industry survey that showed a staggering 90.25% of online entrepreneurs polled saying that they had at least considered creating an online course, and over 34% had at least begun creating one. When we conducted that survey again in late 2016, those numbers had grown even higher; over 50% had started the process of creating their first course (for more data and analysis, see the State of Online Courses appendix at the end of this book).

Even more gratifying to me has been the shift towards providing real education, including support, guidance, and coaching for students as they work through the curriculums that they've signed up for. This is still very much in its infancy, but it bodes well for those educator entrepreneurs, for their students, and for the industry as a whole. Clearly, the entrepreneurial world has caught on to the $100+ billion dollar opportunity that the online learning industry represents!

There's only one problem: seeing the opportunity of effective online education is not at all the same as just "knowing" what it takes to seize it. The big missing piece of the puzzle is understanding how to create and deliver education effectively at scale.

In Summary (TL;DR)

Let's quickly re-cap the most important points from this chapter (not including my thoughts about what it's like to be a new parent; for that, you've got to read the actual chapter!):

- The collision of two worlds – the glacially slow-moving world of education, and the lightning-paced world of online business – is driving the Teach and Grow Rich opportunity. On one hand, formal education has become both ubiquitous and increasingly out of touch with the realities of the modern economy. The implied promise of prosperity from higher education has become a myth.

- On the other hand, online publishing has exploded like the California gold rush. As word of early online publishing successes spread, the idea that anyone with an Internet connection could set up shop and reach the entire world sparked the imaginations of millions, selling digital goods that cost nothing to fulfill.

- This demand created an explosion of opportunity within the cottage industry of information publishing, culminating in the massive launches we see today for multi-thousand-dollar information products.

- The problem is that it doesn't work to provide information without the help or support that people need to truly understand and implement what they're learning. Online entrepreneurs who digitized and automated the teaching process assumed that all the costs of a traditional educational experience (rent, utilities, accreditation, and of course, teachers) are as superfluous to learning as actual paper books are to reading – but they aren't. Digital information may be enough to get you to the point of "knowing," but it usually takes more to get to the point of competent "doing".

- At the heart of the matter are two fundamentally different paradigms of business: publishing vs. education. In a publishing business, your job is to produce something that customers want to buy, and that's it. But that's not how it works in a school or university, because they follow an education paradigm. As long as students live up to what's expected of them, the school has a responsibility to do everything they can to support them, including investing in teachers and support services.

- The current market for digital products will split into two different camps: low-cost information on one side, and premium education on the other. Those businesses that stick to the publishing model will be forced to drop their prices, as the market's willingness to pay inflated prices disappears. We're already seeing this in marketplaces like Amazon, where Kindle books cap out at $30, and Udemy, which has placed a limit on the prices of its video-based products. We're seeing a return to the same long tail distribution where the few mega-hits that sell millions of copies rake in the vast majority of the profits.

- In contrast, those businesses that embrace the paradigm of education will continue to command premium prices, and with increasing ease, as the growing sophistication of the market phases the peddlers of overpriced information out of the picture. Based on our surveys, an increasing number of online entrepreneurs are catching on to this billion-dollar opportunity.

The question is, how do you actually deliver quality education at scale?

Case in Point:
Frank Allgäuer's Journey from Speaker to Author to Online Course Creator

Frank Allgäuer, natural juicing therapist, knows first-hand the difference between information and education.

Frank is a software engineer who's passionate about helping people live more energized lives, primarily through juicing, rebounding, and adopting the right mindset.

He began by delivering live, in-person seminars and talks to groups of 10-30 people. But he found that it was difficult to take the people from listening to actually implementing what they've learned. People who attended his seminars were far from seeing the transformation they wanted.

Because of this, Frank decided to write a book, so people could take the information with them and return to it at their leisure. And so he wrote *Energy Reloaded*, which describes what Frank believes are the three pillars to good health: nutrition, movement, and mindset.

While Frank found the book helpful for reaching certain goals, it still fell short of creating transformation. He thinks the book positioned him as an expert in the field. It also helped him get feedback from his audience through reader reviews.

But while the book was downloaded over 500 times after just a few days of being launched on Amazon, Frank couldn't tell how many read the whole book, much less how many in fact used it to change their lives.

"Someone who just reads a book may not have the mindset to actually put it into action," Frank observed.

That's why Frank decided to create an online course.

"If you have an online course, you can lead the people, guide the people," Frank says. He found that weekly one-hour calls were enough for him to identify his students' pain points "so that they wake up and realize that they have to do something to improve and change their lives."

Those who are enrolled in his online course, in other words, were like the students who received one-on-one tutoring and performed significantly better than those who merely sat in a lecture.

Being able to create this impact in people's lives, Frank says, "is what you can do with an online course and not with a book."

Like Frank, other authors make the jump to become online course creators. They find that, while books make terrific "business cards" and credibility builders, they're not very effective at creating lasting change. An online course, on the other hand, lets creators interact directly with learners and give the level of support needed to achieve the change they were hoping for.

Part 3:
Reimagining Education

"The significant problems of our time won't be solved at the same level of thinking that created them."

- Albert Einstein

In June of 2012, Daphne Koller stepped onto the big red dot that marks center stage at TED, the world's leading conference about big ideas worth spreading.

Her talk, which has since been viewed over 2 million times, was about the promise of online education. She quoted Thomas L. Friedman, who wrote that "big breakthroughs happen when what is suddenly possible meets what is desperately necessary." What is desperately necessary, Koller explained, is for education to be made accessible across geographies and socioeconomic strata. And for the first time, technology made that vision of scalable online education possible.

She painted a near-utopian picture of the future of education, where hundreds of thousands of students could partake in Ivy-league-quality courses for free, from anywhere in the world. It's an inspiring picture that has sparked the imagination of companies (and investors) looking to capitalize on this opportunity, including...

- Udemy, mentioned in the previous chapter (received $113M in investment from 2011 through 2015)

- San Francisco-based CreativeLive (received

$30M in 2012 and 2013)

- Programming education company Treehouse (received $12M from 2011 through 2013)

- Lynda.com, which was acquired by LinkedIn in April of 2015 for a staggering $1.5 billion

Not to mention Koller's own company Coursera, which received $85M from investors in 2012 and 2013.

These companies have done a lot with the money, and delivered on many of the promises that Koller made in her talk. But her most exciting promise remains unfulfilled.

98% Disappointed

In 1974, Garrison Keillor's *A Prairie Home Companion* aired for the first time on Minnesota Public Radio. The show featured a range of music and comedy skits, one of the most well-known being "News from Lake Wobegon", a monologue that would end with the words "Well, that's the news from Lake Wobegon, where all the women are strong, all the men are good looking, and all the children are above average."

Hence the Lake Wobegon Effect, which describes the human tendency to overestimate one's achievements and capabilities relative to others. The phenomenon has been observed in contexts ranging from high school students' appraisal of their leadership skills, drivers' assessment of their driving skills, and many others. The label is poignant, because we all know that everybody can't be above average.

Or can they?

Maybe they can – and that's precisely what Daphne Koller proposed in her talk: to solve the "2 Sigma Problem" posed by educational psychologist Benjamin Bloom back in 1984. Bloom compared students in regular classrooms with students who received 1-on-1 tutoring with "mastery learning" techniques – which just means that they wouldn't move on to new material until mastering the old material. He found that the latter group performed two standard deviations better than students in a traditional lecture-based class (statisticians use the Greek letter sigma to represent standard deviations, hence the "2 Sigma Problem").

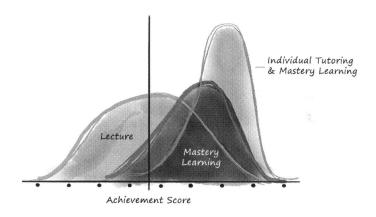

Achievement Score

In Bloom's own words, "the average tutored student was above 98% of the students in the control class." This was a true breakthrough: a way of supporting 98% of students to perform substantially above the current average. The challenge, of course, is in the lack of money and teachers to provide 1-on-1 tutoring to each and every student. The 2 Sigma Problem, then, is to find a way to deliver that support in a way that is scalable and cost-effective.

Which is exactly where Koller closed her TED talk; discussing automated feedback, peer grading, and sophisticated analysis of the homework of hundreds of thousands of students, which in turn allows for the development of even better automated feedback – all in hopes of solving the problem that Bloom presented in 1984. It all sounded great in theory... but how has it panned out?

Not very well, unfortunately. A University of Pennsylvania Graduate School of Education study of a million students enrolled in massively open online courses (MOOCs) found that, on average, only half of those who registered for a course even viewed the first lecture, and only about 4% completed the courses. This in spite of all the sophisticated technology and mechanisms that hundreds of millions of venture-backed dollars can buy. And that doesn't even speak to how those 4% of students actually performed. There are hundreds of studies comparing the outcomes of courses taught in person versus online, and the results have been so consistent as to have arrived at a name for the phenomenon: the "no significant difference" result.

This isn't an indictment of online learning, but rather a recognition that most online learning just isn't designed to provide the support that students truly need to succeed. In fact, the reality is quite the opposite, because for the most part the people tackling the problem aren't the ones who are most likely to be able to solve it. Not because they don't want to, and certainly not because they aren't sufficiently resourced.

On the contrary, it's the hundreds of millions of dollars of venture capital investment that dooms them to failure.

The Strings Attached to a Hundred Million Dollars

Bill Gates has famously said that "automation applied to an inefficient operation will magnify the inefficiency". Well, most attempts at online education are very inefficient, as measured by the proportion of students who actually internalize and apply what they've set out to learn! This isn't a criticism of course creators, who work hard and mean well. It's just an acknowledgement that teaching anything worth learning is a complex endeavor, and it's unlikely that anyone will get it right on their first attempt. While there are a small number of veteran course creators working online, most are new to the craft, adapting their knowledge and curricula to an online course format for the first time. You wouldn't expect someone to hit a home run the first time they step up to the plate, but somehow course creators do expect to get it all right on their first try.

But they won't – even if they have decades of experience teaching the same material in other contexts. That experience helps, of course, but the world of online education comes with its own unique set of challenges and opportunities, including:

- Different learning modalities available to students (text, audio, video, etc.)

- Semi-synchronous access and communication with teachers and other students

- Various degrees of self-pacing available to the student

Not to mention the enormous range of human quirkiness that prevents even offline courses from being a slam dunk 100% of the time. No matter how smart or skilled a course creator you are, expecting to get all of this right on your very first attempt is like the proverbial monkey typing on a keyboard; it just might type Shakespeare, but I wouldn't bet on it!

So what's the solution? Easy, as any software programmer will tell you: first make it work, then make it better. In other words, get a simplified version of it right before adding all the bells and whistles. In some industries, this is referred to as "agile development", and in the world of curriculum design it is known as "formative assessment" – a powerful and sadly underutilized tool that educators can apply to improve student engagement, learner interest, and actual learning results. The key is to get it right on a small scale before taking it to the masses; start with a simple course delivered to a small number of people. Pay attention to what is and isn't working, and evolve your curriculum and delivery plans to make it better the next time around. Test again, learn again, and deploy again, in a cycle of improvement that repeats as often as it takes to get it right.

It's a powerful process... so why isn't it used by the 800-pound gorillas of online education? The reason is simply these tests require students that you can actually interact with and observe. Teachers have known this since time immemorial, because there's no replacement for the insight and perspective a real teacher working with students can gain. If you do enough of that, you'll end up with a curriculum that is tight and efficient enough that you can deliver it at scale, with an affordable level of support (which is not the same as the zero-level of support that most attempts at online teaching involve, putting them squarely on the information side of the information/education divide).

But when you've taken hundreds of millions of a venture capitalist's dollars, you don't have the freedom to leisurely test and iterate. Venture investors live by a mantra of "go big or go home" for very good reason: the degrees of risk involved in funding start-ups make it so that their only chance at turning a profit is if every business they back has the potential for rapid and exponential growth. Because of that, taking a venture investor's money dictates certain strategic choices for your business, the first of which is that you have to scale, and scale fast. The massive investment in testing and iterating is focused on the technology platforms being built, but not on each individual course. Not only that, the courses also need to be cheap (or free), so as to acquire a very large numbers of users in a hurry. This locks you into the long tail economics that work for so few content creators, and reinforces your inability to spend too much time or money on the actual course content.

Now, if you've got content that you can't spend too much time or money refining, and you're selling it cheaply or giving it away for free, what does that look like to you? It's information, not education – clean and clear as day.

That's the paradox of scalable education: that to really deliver quality education at scale, you have to start by investing more time and money in things that don't scale. Not in the delivery platform (which tech start-ups are more than happy to invest in), but in the content itself. Education can absolutely be mass market, but it can't start that way. It's doable, and the opportunity is enormous, but the economic incentives are aligned against venture investors having the appetite or patience to get there, which is why venture-backed companies are unlikely to ever make it happen.

But the good news for most of the people reading this book is that you don't have to worry about that sort of scale, or generating a profitable return on a hundred million dollar investment. For most people, an extra $50,000/year is a fantastic starting point, which is a big part of why the Teach and Grow Rich opportunity is so exciting to so many. Before you can do that, though, your ability to imagine what education can be must be broken free of a prison so insidious that you didn't even realize the bars are there...

Trapped In Yesterday's Classroom

Any creator or consumer of conventional education will agree that it has its fair share of faults. Famed neuroscientist John Medina, author of *Brain Rules*, said it best: "If you wanted to create an education environment that was directly opposed to what the brain was good at doing, you probably would design something like a classroom."

But it also has redeeming characteristics, created by the convergence of students and teacher at a single place and time. This allows them to connect and learn from each other, which can be highly valuable. Unfortunately, those benefits don't translate well to an online setting. So as long as a conventional classroom remains our frame of reference, online education will never be more than a "poor man's version" of a real world classroom. And most of us don't realize just how much that conventional classroom constrains our thinking as to what education can be. We've internalized a long list of assumptions so strongly that it doesn't even occur to us that there are other options. For example, assumptions about the optimal...

- Student to teacher ratio in a classroom (25 students to 1 teacher)

- Distribution of skill levels of students (all students at the same level)

- Length of a lesson or lesson segment (45-60 minutes per session)

- Pace of content delivery (one lesson per week)

- Modality for content delivery (lecture style for the whole class)

- Way to keep students motivated (rewards and punishments)

- Way to evaluate progress and performance (tests and grades)

And that's just the beginning. Most of us have firm implicit assumptions about the answers to all of these things, which are a reflection of our own experiences in educational settings like elementary, secondary, undergraduate, and graduate classrooms. You might be surprised, then, to know that almost all of those assumptions are incorrect (or at least, incorrect for a large portion of students); in some cases, the jury's still out, and in many cases the research has shown conclusively that the way things are conventionally done is appallingly ineffective. But where did all these assumptions come from? Nobody actually set out to create a learning environment that prevents us from learning, so why does education look the way that it does?

The answer is a combination of inertia and economics that govern an in-person classroom; much of what we do started as somebody's best guess, and it's hard to move past that original best guess when practicality and affordability aren't on your side. Case in point: many North American educational settings implicitly assume that a single teacher can handle up to 25 students. This is based on a determination made by the Jewish scholar Maimonides in the 12th century (who, incidentally, taught students in an oral tradition of chanting Torah and engaging in Talmudic studies – not a typical classroom even in the 12th century!). Since then, many scholars of education have made evidence-based arguments for class sizes of 8-12, but still we stick with Maimonides, largely because of the cost and supply of good teachers.

We may roll our eyes at this sort of inertia, but the constraints are real. Even if we know that students would benefit from twice as many qualified teachers than they currently have, that doesn't mean those teachers are available for hire, nor that the money is available to pay them. Research may show that students learn best working at their own pace, but if all the students and teachers have to show up for a lesson to be delivered, there's no choice but to have them all progress as a cohort, rather than as individuals. Hands on interaction with the subject matter might best help us learn, but if that requires access to rare, expensive, or easily damaged equipment, it just isn't practical.

In other words, there are a lot of reasons why most traditional classrooms work the way that they do; some are accidents of history and some are necessities of practicality. That they constrain the future and potential of an entire generation is a tragedy, but that they constrain our imagination as to what education could even look like is a travesty. That's why we must recognize these preconceptions for what they are, set them aside, and reimagine from the ground up what education can be.

How Might We Reimagine Education?

There are myriad ways to reimagine education and do better for our students. They are made possible by the fast-evolving technologies of education delivery, the resourcefulness of enterprising teachers, the increased participation and engagement of students, and the borrowing of best practices from other industries. Taken together, these factors more than level the playing field between traditional education institutions and the independent education entrepreneurs that this book is written for. Here are just a few ideas to whet your appetite and excite your imagination...

- Courses no longer have to be created first and then sold later. The technology that allows for rapid deployment of new content in real-time means that you can develop a curriculum on the fly with the input of your students, to make sure what you're building is exactly aligned with what they want and need. This can be done through live content delivery, or through real-time surveying and adaptation – and as you'll see in later chapters, the counter-intuitive outcome of this "on the fly" development is typically a much better learning experience for the student.

- In the past, curricula had to follow a linear "one size fits all" path from lesson 1 to lesson 2 to lesson 3, simply because if the professor delivers a lecture every week, that's the only way for it to unfold. But now that content can be delivered digitally and virtually, lessons can be laid out in more of a "choose your own adventure" conditional flow-chart pattern; if you already know about this, skip the first lesson, and based on your circumstances choose one of the following three lessons, etc. These paths can be pre-determined, or can be chosen and adjusted in real-time based on a student's comfort level with whatever they happen to be learning in the moment.

- If both teacher and students must converge at the same place and time for a lecture to be delivered, all parties needed to be able to plan for arrival and departure... hence the fixed standard length of a lesson. But the reality is that some content needs longer treatment, and some needs much shorter, which is possible when students and teacher can be untethered from each other. Just as cable television shows are all 42 minutes long (an hour minus commercials), while Netflix original episodes can be whatever length the content and story calls for, so too will education get better as the constraints of arbitrary lesson lengths become irrelevant.

- Similarly, technology-based delivery of content means that rather than dripping a course out to all participants on an approximation of the average student's best schedule, students can progress at their own pace by "gating" the delivery of new content based on demonstrated understanding of what has already been delivered. This is called a mastery approach to learning in education circles, and it is responsible for the first standard deviation jump in results for Benjamin Bloom's research participants that we discussed earlier in this chapter. Finally, technology has made it practical to deliver at scale.

- In the wise words sometimes credited to Benjamin Franklin, "Tell me and I forget, teach me and I may remember, involve me and I will learn." One of the best ways to involve someone in the content is by teaching it and evaluating the work of others. Creative use of peer grading systems in which students give each other feedback is not only a great way of improving the internalization of the subject matter, but also a great way of scaling the delivery of meaningful feedback to all students. While some educators worry that peer grading is just a matter of the blind leading the blind, research has shown that when implemented correctly, the feedback is just as accurate and helpful as the teacher would provide, and the process of giving that feedback becomes one of the most valuable parts of the learning process.

- Gamification technologies are still in their infancy, but already there are fascinating opportunities for integrating a mix of tracking, feedback, community, and incentives into educational experiences that make the learning process more engaging and experiential, leading to higher levels of educational content consumption and internalization, which in turns leads to higher student completion and success rates.

As you can see, the motivated entrepreneurial educator's palette of possibilities is almost endless (for more ideas and inspiration, visit http://www.ted.com/playlists/24/re_imagining_school). And just as with any palette, the key isn't to use every color with every brush stroke, but rather to use the right ones in just the right places, for maximum effect. You don't need them all to get started – on the contrary, the path to starting your own education empire has never been more straight-forward or accessible, which is exactly what we'll explore in the next part of this book.

In Summary (TL;DR)

Let's quickly re-cap the most important points from this chapter (not including all the takeaways from my favorite TED talk; for that, you've got to read the actual chapter!):

- The promise of online education, where hundreds of thousands of students from anywhere in the world can partake in Ivy-league-quality education for free, has sparked the imaginations of companies and investors, to the tune of hundreds of millions of dollars.

- The most exciting promise of online education, however, is to solve the "2 Sigma Problem" of providing a level of support that would help 98% of students perform above average, in a way that is scalable and cost-effective. But that promise has so far gone unfulfilled, because of the inefficiency of most attempts at online education. This isn't a criticism of course creators, who work hard and mean well. It's an acknowledgement that teaching anything worth learning is complex, and the possibility of doing it online is too new for anyone to be an expert at it yet.

- The solution? First make it work, then make it better. Known as "agile development" in the tech industry and "formative assessment" in education, this underutilized tool can be applied by educators to improve student engagement, interest, and learning. The key is to get it right on a small scale before taking it to the masses.

Start with a simple course delivered to a small number of people, pay attention to what is and isn't working, and change your curriculum and delivery plans to make it better the next time around. Keep testing, learning, and deploying in a cycle of improvement.

- The paradox of scalable education is that, to deliver education at scale, you have to invest more time and money in things that don't scale: not in the delivery platform, but in the content itself.

- To reimagine education, we must break free of our assumptions about what makes for effective education inside a classroom. Many of the traditional classroom practices are based on incorrect best guesses that have persisted due to inertia and economics.

- There are many ways to reimagine education to do better for our students, including: developing a curriculum on the fly with the input of your students; delivering lessons in more of a conditional flow-chart pattern rather than one-size-fits-all curricula; making course content as long or as short as is called for; facilitating peer review to improve the internalization of the subject matter as well as to scale the delivery of meaningful feedback to all students; and, using gamification for tracking, feedback, community, and incentives to make the learning process more engaging and experiential.

- These innovations stretch the impact and income that an education empire can create, but you don't need them all to get started. On the contrary, the path to starting your own education empire has never been more straightforward.

We'll explore that path in the next part of this book...

Case in Point:
Sean Platt's Apprentice Program
for Writers

Sean Platt is a bestselling independent author who, along with his business partners, provides an eight-month apprentice program for aspiring self-published authors.

The program helps writers come up with their own repeatable process for writing and publishing a bestselling book, from finding a niche full of hungry readers, to packaging and launching their book.

Sean and his partners came up with their program, because there was nowhere else for people to go and learn the combination of craft and commerce, and be nurtured through what Sean and his team call "experiential education."

"It really needs to be hands-on. It needs to be tangible," Sean explains, "We need to anchor lessons with memory, which is why we try to do stuff in person as often as possible, or in small groups. We want people to think about what they're doing. We want to ask questions."

The apprentice program isn't just a bunch of videos to watch and check off. Instead, it focuses on anchoring lessons with experience, so that they become a memory for the apprentices.

Another way the program is doubling down on providing real education is by differentiating the education. For example, Sean and his partners noticed that some of their students were beginners, while others were more advanced. Instead of attending the same workshops, they self-identify either as beginner or advanced, and then are directed to the appropriate workshop.

Sean sees a big difference in the results of their apprentices compared to those who go through other writers' courses. The "hands-on" approach helps them to figure out how to do things. "It has really closed the loops for them," Sean says.

Another key difference Sean has observed is the strong sense of community among those who are going through the program at the same time: "There's just a real give and take and back and forth that I never saw in high school at all, or in any part of school, and definitely not in a lot of the info products I've seen online."

Between the program's general calls and genre-specific calls, "you have a lot of mixing and matching, and a lot of sharing of ideas. No one is afraid to ask questions. No one is afraid to admit when they need help. That dynamic community is kind of amazing. That's just the opposite of everything I've seen with download-this-and-consume-it," Sean says.

Part 4:
Profile of an
Educator Entrepreneur

"If someone offers you an amazing opportunity and you're not sure you can do it, say yes - then learn how to do it later."

-Richard Branson

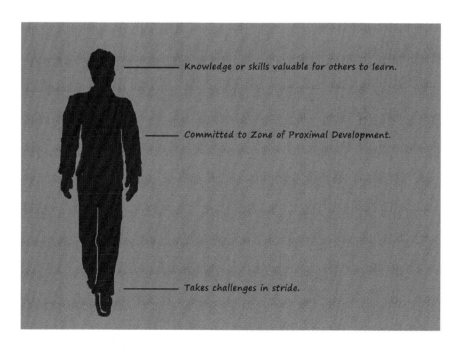

So far, we've talked about the Teach and Grow Rich opportunity in the broad sense; what it is, where it came from, and what makes it special. We explored the three unique characteristics of this opportunity that make it unlike almost any other:

1. Democratized access for anyone who has knowledge or skills that others might value (which is basically everyone).

2. Fat tail economics that allow us all to do well financially without having to create a mega-hit or emerge as a market leader.

3. The opportunity to grow rich by creating positive impact for those that we care about serving.

Then we dug deeper, into the historical context from which this opportunity emerged, as well as the implications that this is so much more than just another business opportunity. Sure, it's an accessible path to the freedom and wealth that so many of us crave, and that might be enough to warrant careful attention. But even more importantly, the Teach and Grow Rich opportunity will be a driving force of change in our world, by providing the benefit of high value education to so many who need it so desperately. There's money to be earned, freedom to be had, and impact to be made.

Now it's time to shift gears, and talk about how to seize this opportunity in a way that is realistic and tangible. To do all this, what actions have to be taken? What strategies have to be followed? And, first things first: what sort of person can really succeed here? Could it be someone like you?

Four Kinds of Educator Entrepreneurs... Which Are You?

The one bar that you need to pass to succeed with the Teach and Grow Rich opportunity is that you must have knowledge or skills that are valuable for others to learn. So long as that's true, it doesn't matter if you're the world's leading authority in your field, or have just been dabbling in it for a few years. Nor does it matter whether you've ever been paid for this expertise or not, how much teaching skill or experience you have. It doesn't even matter whether you have a powerful marketing platform, or none at all. The only non-negotiable requirement for success with the Teach and Grow Rich opportunity is that you know something that others would benefit from learning. If you meet that single requirement, this opportunity for income through impact is yours to seize.

That doesn't mean the path to success will look the same for everyone, though. Your track record in your field and the degree of expertise you bring to the table aren't deal-breakers for your success, but they will influence the path that you will take to get to where you want to go. In my experience working with thousands of aspiring educator entrepreneurs, I've seen four major kinds of course creators who consistently find their way to success: the Professionals, the Journeymen, the Experts, and the Insiders:

- **The Professionals** have already acquired status in their field that translates into authority and income. They're recognized as leaders in their industries, charging a premium for their time and insights. Typical examples are high-priced consultants, coaches, technicians, and speakers. Their expertise already generates a comfortable income, but they are trapped trading time for money... even if it is a lot of money! They might yearn to take a sabbatical without a precipitous dip in income, or they might be dreaming of making their living without having to get on so many airplanes. Or maybe they just want to reach and impact more people than they can serve personally. The Teach and Grow Rich opportunity makes all of this possible.

- **The Journeyman** doesn't have the depth of experience that the Professional does, but is in the trenches working in their respective fields. This knowledge and experience is valuable to others who want to learn. Typical examples are consultants and coaches who are earlier in their careers, and "side hustlers" working on their business or passion project while holding a day job; they may not be at the top of their fields, but they know their stuff and have made money doing it, often for years. Their challenge is to increase both their income and their impact. The Teach and Grow Rich opportunity is the path to doing both, by serving others who wish to learn what the Journeyman already knows.

- **The Experts** have a deep passion for their field, making them recognized experts on the topic. That passion and expertise isn't necessarily linked to their work, though, nor is it necessarily producing an income. Typical examples are university professors, researchers, authors, and bloggers – people who possess a deep passion and knowledge of their field, but whose income may not reflect their depth of expertise. They've been told that "if you do what you love, the money will follow", but so far it hasn't. The Teach and Grow Rich opportunity is a scalable and sustainable way of changing that, once and for all.

- **The Insider** doesn't have the deep experience or credentials of the Expert, but rather a serious engagement with a field that gives them an inside view and perspective that newcomers lack, and would benefit from. These are the hobbyists, enthusiasts and aficionados; not experts, but people who possess both the knowledge and the passion to help newcomers to a field take their first intrepid steps. This is the fourth grader teaching the second grader – multiplying income and impact in the process through the Teach and Grow Rich opportunity. Often, when someone thinks of themselves as having nothing to teach, they later discover that they're an excellent Insider, with corresponding insights to share.

People who fit one of these four profiles of course creator can look forward to a great deal of success with the Teach and Grow Rich opportunity. Each of them will follow a slightly different path to achieving that success, but it is within all of their reach to attain it. You probably recognize yourself in one (or possibly several!) of these categories, but if you want more certainty about which kind of educator entrepreneur you are (and the strengths and opportunities that it implies for you), you're invited to take the free assessment that my team of course building coaches has developed, located at http://mrse.co/profile.

Whatever kind of entrepreneur you are, there is ample room for you to succeed with the Teach and Grow Rich opportunity, using the methodology laid out over the rest of these pages. I've seen this to be true over and over again, despite some of the common reasons people imagine will keep them from achieving that success.

"But What If... [Insert Excuse Here]"

In teaching about this opportunity, I typically hear three broad reasons why people fear they might not be successful as an educator entrepreneur:

1. Lack of credentials or expert status
2. Lack of a teaching background
3. Lack of platform or marketing experience

While these are all nice-to-haves, no single one or even all of them together need to be deal-breakers, so long as they're approached in the right way. Let's explore why these three concerns don't hold water:

Why You Don't Need
Credentials or Expert Status

Almost thirty years ago, clinical psychologists Pauline R. Clance and Suzanne A. Imes coined the term "imposter syndrome" to describe high achievers who don't feel like they're really qualified for the success that they've created. It's the Lake Wobegon Effect in reverse: rather than over-estimating their abilities, the Imposter Syndrome means that many of us have trouble accepting the credit that we actually deserve. This is very common with entrepreneurs, and can often manifest as a feeling of "I'm not good enough to do this; who am I to be teaching, when others are more qualified?"

In my experience, this question is a red herring. Not because "you don't need to know anything to build a course", as some might claim – of course you need to know things! As I wrote earlier, the one non-negotiable requirement for success with the Teach and Grow Rich opportunity is that you must have knowledge or skills that are valuable to others to learn (and I'll show you how to zero in on exactly what that might be for you in the next chapter).

Assuming you have that knowledge or skill, though, credentials don't really matter, because credentials have only ever been a short-hand way of communicating that you have a certain skill or expertise. In other words, it's not the credential as an engineer that people care about *per se*, but rather the confidence that credential gives them that buildings you design won't fall down. If you feel legitimately confident in your knowledge and abilities, then you just need to find an alternate way of giving your prospective students that confidence. There are lots of ways of doing that, ranging from a demonstration of your expertise (people believe their eyes more than they believe credentials anyway), endorsements from people you've helped, results you feel confident enough to guarantee, etc.

Once people feel confident in the outcome that you promise you can deliver, they won't care about the credential, or lack thereof. I realize that this runs counter to what a lot of people have been taught and trained to believe about the importance and value of credentials. But there are just too many examples in too many fields of the highest paid experts often being those who are the least formally credentialed. Now, that isn't to say that credentials aren't an advantage; of course they are. They just aren't a necessity – especially if you've spent decades in your field developing a deep knowledge that has never been reflected in a formal certification. It's also true if you're the proverbial fourth grader who is the expert to the second grader: so long as you know enough to help your students, who cares what else you do or don't know, or have or haven't done?

The bottom line is that very few are the people who care about raw knowledge for it's own sake. What really matters to most students is the outcome that the knowledge will give them. That's as much a function of what you teach as how you teach it. Which brings us to our second area of concern: what if I don't have experience teaching?

Why You Don't Need
a Teaching Background

Even more than credentials in a specific subject area, many believe that the only people who should be building courses are trained and experienced teachers. While teaching experience is definitely a "nice-to-have", though ,it isn't a "must" for aspiring educator entrepreneurs. There are two big reasons why this is true: a much more limited scope of teaching than most educational contexts, and the iterative course creation methodology that I'll share with you in the next chapter of this book.

With regards to scope, remember that we're talking about building a very tightly focused, outcome-driven course that can ideally be delivered in weeks or months. This is not a general education experience spanning months or years! Given that, that the scope of knowledge necessary to deliver such a course is much more narrow that in most teaching situations, where you need to be able to impart a wide array of subject knowledge to a wide array of students. This makes it feasible for new teachers to get their heads around what it will take to deliver it well. To continue the analogy from earlier, the fourth grader is the expert to the second grader, but that doesn't mean the fourth grader can teach the entire second grade! As long as you stay tightly focused on a topic and outcome, you'll be fine learning the teaching skills you need as you develop and deliver your courses.

Just as important, Teach and Grow Rich is more than just an opportunity; it is also a methodology, laid out in detail in the next chapter of this book. When followed correctly, it creates a lot more room for aspiring course creators to learn as they go, and develop the teaching abilities that they need in real-time based on feedback and input from their students. The process that I'll share with you creates a lot of room for iteration and course correction along the way. The road might be a little bumpier, but if you're willing to endure the short-term discomfort, you can acquire the teaching skills that you need as you go. All you need is a clear picture of what you'll teach (which we'll get to in the next chapter), and students who want to learn. Which brings us to the last point of concern for many aspiring course creators: what if I don't have the following or marketing skills to get this off the ground?

Why You Don't Need
a Platform or Marketing Experience

When it comes to the world of online business, the biggest dividing line between the haves and the have nots is marketing skill, and the platform and resources that tend to come with it. As a skilled marketer, selling anything is easier, and you know how to attract an audience and build a platform. This in turn makes it even easier to sell things, which gives you even more resources to grow your audience – and so on, and so forth. It's a virtuous cycle that works beautifully for the people who are positioned to take advantage of it.

But what if you don't have those skills, or those resources? What if you aren't a natural marketer, don't feel comfortable selling things, and haven't built an email list of people who want to buy things from you? If that sounds like you, and it gives you pause about what your prospects are for online business success, then you aren't alone! It's a legitimate concern, exacerbated by the information products promising a rags-to-riches transformation that we talked about earlier in this book.

The fact is, though, that every single person who has an audience or platform today had to build it from nothing. Sure, some modern success stories came from a place of money and natural talent, but many didn't. While some successful online business owners have past successes to point to, more of us have past failures that we had to recover from. Marketing, like any other skill, is something that can be learned, and many of the people who are great at it today grew their skill level from a starting point somewhere between mediocre and miserable. Would it be nice to skip that learning process and start your course building journey as a marketing expert with a loyal following? Of course. But that expertise and following are absolutely a nice-to-have, rather than a necessity for creating a successful online education business.

Just like deep credentials and teaching experience, a lack of marketing skill can be overcome... especially because marketing isn't actually as important to long-term online business success as most people think it is. On balance, the better your product (i.e. your course) is, and the better the outcomes it creates for your students, the more you'll be able to lean on actual results rather than slick marketing to attract new students. Marketing matters most in the short-term, and the process and methodology laid out in the next chapter will help you overcome that challenge. As long as you have a mindset of learning and growth, the path ahead will be bright – even when it may not seem that way at first.

Committing to the Zone (of Proximal Development)

Most tasks fall into two broad categories: the things that we are capable of doing, and the things that we aren't. Thankfully, there's a third category, and therein lies our potential for development and growth: the things that we can do with some outside help and support. Almost a century ago, Soviet psychologist Lev Vygotsky described that third category as the Zone of Proximal Development: tasks difficult enough that we couldn't reliably do them on our own, but that we could successfully complete with the guidance and support of a capable teacher or peer. And if you spend time in that Zone with support, something magical happens: things that used to be difficult or impossible start becoming with easy reach!

103

The single most important ingredient to your success as a course builder (or anything else in life, really) – more than any other skill or ability – will be a good teacher, and the willingness to dwell in the state of mild discomfort that characterizes your Zone of Proximal Development, just beyond your comfort zone. No matter how capable or skilled you may be, without that willingness and support your talents are fixed at their current level. It isn't always pleasant to operate beyond our comfort zone (in fact, it is uncomfortable, by definition!), but only there do we learn new skills and acquire new abilities.

And the good news is that we all have plenty of experience operating there, because it is where we learned everything that was once difficult, but now comes easily. The greatest success and achievements for all of us lie in the areas that we have not yet mastered. This is true in all areas of life, and especially on your journey to becoming an educator entrepreneur, that will involve a number of new skills to master and positions to put yourself in, including:

- Researching to see what the market wants to learn that you can teach

- Telling people about your course for the first time

- Setting up the technologies for collecting payment

- Standing in front of a room (literal or virtual) and teaching

- Supporting students that are stuck or don't get it

- Dealing with students who are challenged and frustrated

- Adapting when technologies don't work as expected

Obviously, this is a very partial list, and in no particular order. Now, all of these challenges can be overcome, and none of them needs to be particularly difficult, provided you have the right guide to follow. The key, though, is the realistic expectation that some parts of the process will challenge you. If you have that expectation, you'll take the challenges in stride as they come. Without that expectation, though, each challenge runs the risk of derailing you. In all of my experience working with aspiring course creators and online entrepreneurs, every single one experienced challenges along the way. Every. Single. One. And all those who went on to be successful pushed through those challenges and kept on going. It's just what it takes to be successful, and it's what you need to model for your own students to be successful, too. That willingness to truly commit to the Zone of Proximal Development, more than anything else, is what characterizes the profile of a successful education entrepreneur.

In Summary (TL;DR)

Okay, let's quickly re-cap the most important points from this chapter:

- The only non-negotiable requirement for success with the Teach and Grow Rich opportunity is to have knowledge or skills that would be valuable to others to learn.

- From my experience, there are four major groups of successful course creators, each with different levels of expertise, authority, and degree to which they have monetized their knowledge: The Professionals, the Journeymen, the Experts, and the Insiders.

- The three most common reasons why people don't think they will succeed as an educator entrepreneur are: lack of credentials or expert status, lack of a teaching background, and lack of platform or marketing experience. None of these can in fact keep one from succeeding as an educator entrepreneur.

- More than any other skill or ability, the most important ingredients to your success as a course builder are a good teacher and the willingness to dwell in the Zone of Proximal Development (or the level of difficulty which you can perform with the guidance and support of a capable teacher or peer), no matter how difficult or uncomfortable it gets.

If that sounds good to you, then read on, because the next step is the co-creation of your own course!

Case in Point:
Arantxa Mateo, the Unexpected
Weight Loss Teacher

When it comes to weight loss, it would have traditionally taken millions of dollars and superstar status for somebody to penetrate the market. But not with the Teach and Grow Rich opportunity. Arantxa Mateo is a weight loss coach whose mission is to help people lose weight safely, effectively, and sustainably.

However, before becoming an online course creator, she struggled with trading her hours for dollars. In the first place, she had a hard time finding enough clients to reach her income goals. And because she could provide one-on-one coaching to only so many people, her income and impact were limited by how many clients she could give individual attention to.

Although she wanted to leverage the internet to coach more people, Arantxa didn't think she had enough of a platform to teach online. She didn't have a mailing list, a huge social media following, a significant marketing budget—not even a Kindle ebook on the topic. In the beginning of her journey as educator entrepreneur, she worried about not having an online audience to speak of. How could she make a dent in this crowded and hyper-competitive industry? My advice to Arantxa: "Just trust the system because it works."

Driven by the desire to expand her reach as well as to counteract false and harmful information about weight loss, she decided to give the course co-creation process a fair try. Even though she had neither prominence nor an audience when she began, she enrolled five people into her pilot course for $197 each. That's all she needed to prove to herself that she could make a reasonable income from online courses. Sure, she would never get as big as Weight Watchers, but she didn't have or want to be that big to achieve what she considers a "rich" life.

After running her pilot online course, Arantxa realized how fulfilling it is to share her knowledge with students while creating products she can sell again and again.

Part 5:
Co-Creating Your Course

"Alone we can do so little; together we can do so much."

-Helen Keller

"Measure twice, cut once" is a great maxim for carpenters... but in business things are sometimes a little more complicated. The biggest difference is in carpentry all the pertinent dimensions and materials lend themselves to easy measurement. In business, much of what we'd most like to validate and quantify is hard to do without testing the market with a real offer. This is true of factors external to the entrepreneur and business, like what the market wants and is willing to pay for, and for things inside the heart and mind of the entrepreneur, like what they will find most rewarding.

But business is risky. There's the practical risk of investing your time, energy, and money in something that may or may not pan out. And there's also the personal risk making yourself vulnerable by putting yourself and your ideas out for the world to judge as it sees fit. This leads to a very understandable inclination to de-risk the process, further reinforced by business thought leaders who exhort us to make every effort to find our deep inner "why" to drive all else in our endeavors. This idea is both compelling and well-received; Simon Sinek's famous "Start With Why" TEDx talk, for example, is one of the most popular TED videos ever published, with nearly 30 million views on their website alone. The pinnacle of this find-your-deep-purpose movement is in the growing popularity of the Japanese concept of ikigai, loosely translated as "a reason for being". It lies at the crossroads of four questions:

1. What do I love?

2. What am I great at?

3. What does the world need?

4. What could I be paid for?

Any single answer that can be given to all four of these questions is your ikigai, which will bring great satisfaction and meaning to your life. According to the Japanese, everyone has an ikigai, and finding it requires a deep and often lengthy search of self.

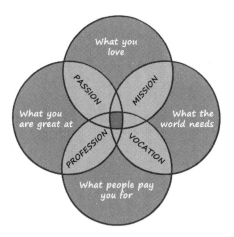

This ideology drives many would-be online entrepreneurs and course creators, who misunderstand both its purpose, and the way to arrive at the best answer for you. They seek to figure out exactly what their market opportunity-aligned deep purpose and mission is before putting anything out into the world, but that's not how these things work in real life. The reason is simple: these frameworks work best as a vehicle for reflecting on and evaluating experiences that you've already had, rather than imagining ones that you haven't. They are tools for focusing, but when taken out of context and applied to try and find the single best work to pursue without real world experience, the search for this insight is more likely to become a vehicle for procrastination than anything else. Very simply, as attractive as we might find the idea of arriving at the perfect answer through deep soul searching that requires no real-world risk or skinning of knees, the search for that deep meaning can only be successful when informed by real world interactions and experiences.

Ikigai is a great ideal to aspire to, but best path to reach it is to set it aside temporarily, and focus on the nearest and most accessible opportunity for you to put a course out into the world. Not something that you will necessarily teach and evolve for years and decades to come, but something that will let you get your feet wet with your first foray into meaningful work with students, who can provide you with real feedback as to whether what you're offering is valuable enough for them to want to pay for it.

Choosing Your Course Topic: Where Interest Meets Opportunity

Finding one's Ikigai is counsel of unreasonable perfection, and finding your why is best accomplished by putting something out into the world without overthinking it, to see both how it is received and how you feel teaching it. Given that, how do you as an aspiring educator entrepreneur set out to find what you should teach on your way to growing rich?

In many cases, the answer is right under your nose, in the experiences that you've already had engaging with ideas and helping the people around you. After all, every person reading this book has had their fair share of life experiences and lessons learned in the years that have led up to this moment. Some of those might prove valuable to others, and some of them very likely already have. So begin there: a mental review of the places you've been, the things you've done, and the people you've interacted with over the last two or three years. Look especially for the people in your past whom you've helped in a way that they truly appreciated. What did you help them with? What did you teach them? What were the outcomes that they found to be most valuable?

You'll want to get very specific very soon, but for right now all we need is the broad, high-level topic. Think "finance", "fashion", "food", or something equally broad in scope. You'll want to filter these topics through two questions:

1. **"Does this topic align with an expertise that I'm at least somewhat known for?"** – We don't usually get good enough at something to teach it without some sort of background with the subject matter, and that sort of background will often leave clues in the form of past experiences, successes, and maybe even credentials. In many cases the area of expertise will be at least

somewhat focused, niched, or unusual.

2. **"Is this topic of interest and value to people that I can reach with relative ease?"** – This is an important reality check for aspiring course creators, because it's hard to get good at something without being at all connected to anyone who stands to benefit from that expertise. This skill assessment allows us to validate that we're on track with a topic area that will truly be of value to the market – after all, it's a lot easier to find out if you're on track if there are prospective students to whom you can easily present your course idea, and see if they bite.

Now, what if you don't meet these criteria? What if you want to build a course about a skill or talent that you aren't yet known for, or aspire to reach a market that you thus far haven't had any contact with? This is still do-able, but it will be a longer and more difficult process. In this scenario, you're energies are probably best invested in the short-term by acquiring that expertise and developing that network of relationships, rather than building a course.

The good news is that for almost everybody I've encountered, there are topics that do meet these criteria that are within their immediate grasp. And often, they are best served pursuing one of those accessible ideas, to build their course building muscles, and start generating an income that will fund their future growth in new directions.

Remember, all you want at this point is a broad, high-level topic, like "finance", "fashion", "food", or something equally broad in scope. Armed with that high-level topic of focus to teach, the next step is to zero in to something narrow and specific that you can teach – and that can lead to meaningful outcomes for your students – in a short amount of time.

Zeroing In:
The Two-Hour Plane Ride

The path to success with the Teach and Grow Rich opportunity is very different from the "get rich online" mythology. We all might enjoy daydreaming from time to time about conceiving of a course, launching it into the world, and being met by ever growing waves of critical acclaim and success. Eventually, though, the time comes to wake up and work on our real businesses. When that happens, wise entrepreneurs know that even their best guess as to what the market really wants may not be a true reflection of reality.

The only way to know for sure is to test. Your first course – which we call a "pilot" course – should be designed to validate a few basic assumptions as quickly and inexpensively as possible. Quickly, so that you can pivot and iterate rapidly as the situation calls for, and inexpensively, so as to minimize the risk to the entrepreneur. The assumptions that must be validated are that your promised outcome:

1. Is valuable enough to your market that they are happy to pay for it, and

2. That you can deliver it at or above the levels that
   you claim.

Neither of these goals – speed and low cost – is met by the
ambitions of most first-time course creators, who want to
teach everything about everything that relates to their topic
area, and wind up with plans for a massive, six-month or
year-long course. That sort of course takes ages to produce,
which means a very long timeline to gaining real knowledge
about whether the market actually wants it. The broad
focus of such a mega-course means that while it's somewhat
valuable to a lot of people, it isn't very valuable to anyone,
which makes it very hard to sell. And if the course does
somehow attract students, and those students struggle
to get to the finish line (which is very likely on the first
iteration of any course, for reasons explained earlier in this
book), the giant scope makes it very difficult to diagnose
what exactly went wrong – nor is it easy to discover what
can be done differently or better in the future. This isn't
the final, extended *magnum opus* that you might one day
create. Rather, it's the minimum viable version for you to
get outside validation that you're on the right track.

So how do you find an appropriate level of focus for your
pilot course, that will validate that you've hit on an outcome
that people will pay for, and that you can deliver?

An easy way to zero in on an appropriate level of focus
involves a thought exercise about a short plane ride from
New York to Chicago. Imagine, if you will, that you arrive
at the airport, go through security, and board your plane.
You find your seat and fasten your seatbelt. After the flight

attendant has pointed out the door you just came in through and explained how to fasten the seatbelt you've already fastened, the plane takes off and you're on your way. Just as the plane starts taxiing down the runway, you start chatting with the person sitting next to you. You immediately hit it off, and learn that they are your ideal prospect and in dire need of your help. You've got the length of the flight, which is just over two hours long, to teach them as much as you can to provide that help and transform their lives. So what would you teach in those two hours that will create the biggest impact in their lives?

This thought exercise is useful in arriving at a focus for your pilot course because it crystallizes your thinking around the minimum viable outcome that you can deliver that would still be meaningfully impactful to your students. You can then test your hypothesis in relatively short order, and maximize your chances of success by co-creating as much of the curriculum as possible with your actual students. But before you can engage students as co-creators of your pilot course, you need at least a one-page outline of what you'll teach them.

Your One-Page Pilot Course Outline

A one-page outline may seem unreasonably sparse, and it stands in sharp contrast to what many first-time course creators do, which is to spend months mapping out detailed scripts of every word they are going to say. But a long and detailed script is a terrible idea for a couple of reasons.

First of all, it isn't likely to create a good experience for your students. Even if you know your subject matter, that doesn't mean you know how to teach it in this kind of course format, because you haven't done it before. Since this is a new experience, you don't know where your students might be confused, or get stuck, or need help. The more rigid and detailed your curriculum plan, the harder it will be to diverge from it when your students need you to. On the other hand, a co-created curriculum and learning experience (as you'll learn how to deliver later in this chapter) will be a lot better for your students, and for you, too.

Beyond these disadvantages to your students, the business logistics of developing a longer script mean that the longer you spend preparing, the longer it will take you to launch. The longer it takes you to launch, the more inertia can tend to set in, and the more likely it is that life will get in the way.

The solution is to prepare in advance only what you need to enroll your co-creating students, which can usually be achieved by mapping out what you intend to teach in a single page. This outline should only take you a few hours to create; make a list of the big topics that you need to cover, and each of them will be a lesson. Under each of those topics, add a handful of bullets about the specific things you will talk about. This is enough of an outline for you to be able to sell your pilot course with – and once you've sold it, you will spend a little more time fleshing out each lesson, and perhaps designing some high-level handouts, worksheets, etc.

Now, you might feel that this is a scant preparation, and you'd be right – except that you're already coming to the table with a wealth of expertise. Remind yourself of your expertise in this subject matter. All you need at this stage is a high-level overview of what concepts you will teach to your students and in what order. The specifics of how to teach them are best co-created with your students live, in real-time, informed by the in-the-moment reactions and responses of your students. Detailed scripts or slides prepared in advance of that input are unlikely to be well aligned with what your students will actually need in the moment.

If this makes you a little uncomfortable, that's okay – remember the importance of stepping out of your comfort zone and operating in your Zone of Proximal Development. It can be uncomfortable, but this method allows you to adjust, pivot, and iterate, to create the best experience for your students. It will also inform the creation of your final (non-pilot) course further down the line, which is when you'll take everything that you learned in the pilot and turn it into high quality videos and other materials.

The one-page outline is all you need to attract students, and once you have them you'll be able to develop the curriculum with them in real-time. Counter-intuitively, this real-time development is critical to the creation of a curriculum that best serves your students. We'll explore that further, but first, you'll need students to teach...

The IKEA Effect and the Magic of Co-Creation

In July of 2012, Michael I. Norton of Harvard Business School, Daniel Mochon of Yale University, and Dan Ariely of Duke University published an article in the Journal of Consumer Psychology, describing a phenomenon that they called the IKEA Effect.

They discovered this phenomenon by conducting a series of experiments in which a group of test subjects were given the task of building or creating something. They ran experiments where the participants built things out of Lego blocks, or folded origami figures, or assembled IKEA boxes – which is where the experiment got its name. Once the participants were finished, they were asked how much they would pay for whatever it was that they built. Then the researchers got a new group of people and showed them what the previous group had built, and asked what they would be willing to pay for those same objects.

In essence, they compared – through scientific and statistically valid methods – how valuable people perceive things that they make as compared with things made by others. The results showed unequivocally that people place a lot more value on things they were involved in creating than on things made by somebody else. And the more involved they are in the creation, the more they value what is ultimately produced.

This research has important implications about your pilot

courses; both how you will deliver them, and especially the way in which you will enroll paying students (and overcome any lack of marketing ability or resources). Consider, for a moment, the relationship you have with most products and services you see advertised. It's hard, isn't it? The truth is that we don't have much of a relationship with most of the things we think about buying, because whatever it is, somebody else created it for their own reasons. We hope that it'll be helpful and valuable to us, but if we find something that could be a little better or cheaper, then we'll just go with that option instead.

If you've already bought it, though, it's a different story. Your experience with what you've bought, and its impact on your life, create a narrative that makes it special and unique – and if the experience has been positive, then you'll probably be loyal to the product. Maybe you've heard the marketing truism that a customer who has already bought something from you is eight times more likely to buy again than a stranger is to make their first purchase? Well, that's because of the narrative of relationship that your customers have with you, which strangers don't. It's the Cocktail Party Effect, applied to business. You know how when you're at a party, there are a dozen conversations going on and it's hard to focus on any one of them? But the moment someone mentions you, your ears and brain zero in on that conversation and ignore all the rest. That's what co-creation does for you and your business, by making your audience a part of the narrative of your offer's creation. As you continue to share the story, they perk up and pay attention because it's their story, too.

That's the power of the piloting process described in this

chapter; it makes your audience part of the creation of your pilot course, which gives you an advantage even stronger than a list of paying customers. Incidentally, this process can only really be applied if you're willing and able to start with smaller pilots, which is another reason why the large companies we looked at in the previous chapter just can't play this game. But you can – by asking your prospects for their input before you create your offer, and then asking the people who sign up for more input as you deliver your pilot to them so you can make it better. This puts the IKEA Effect into play by making your whole audience a part of creating your offer, regardless of whether they buy your pilot (which many will), or whether they aren't ready yet; either way, they'll be bound to you in a powerful way that most other businesses just can't compete with, and that sets you up for success in the short-term and in the long-term. Now let's turn our attention to how you can specifically apply it to attract paying students into your first pilot course.

The Mechanics of Co-Creation, a.k.a. How to Sell Your Pilot

So we've finally come to the million dollar question: how do you actually enroll paying students into your pilot course before you've even built it? And how do you do it without turning into a pushy sales person or giving your nearest and dearest the impression that you've just joined some sort of network marketing fad? There are two answers to this question: the one that a lot of people want to hear, and the real one.

The wished for answer is one that offers a process that doesn't cost much or any money, reaches an infinite quantity of prospective students, and convinces them to sign up and pay you money without you ever having to do anything uncomfortable like get on the phone and talk to them. Essentially, it's a magical internet "easy button"; the idea that if you hit on just the right strategy with just the right technologies and platforms, internet riches are yours. Obviously, there's no such easy button that I can offer you – but you already knew that, right?

The real answer involves stepping into your Zone of Proximal Development, and doing things that are sometimes uncomfortable. You'll have to walk before you run; start with people who already like and trust you, before reaching out to strangers. And actually talk to people, so that you can learn what language and ideas they respond to the best, and get feedback as to why they might not be responding at all. The process that I'll lay out won't sound sexy the way that some hit or miss "viral social media" strategy might, but it will have the benefit of actually working (I've seen it happen for thousands of course creators, many of whose stories are shared in the appendix at the end). And it will create a foundation for larger successes that will follow.

Let's dive in, starting with being very clear about the scope of what we want to accomplish: the goal right now isn't to attract hundreds or thousands (or hundreds of thousands!) of students to your course. That will happen eventually, but you aren't there yet. Right now the goal is to attract anywhere from a handful to a few dozen students to your pilot course. With them, you can validate that the direction you've chosen is valuable enough to your market that they are happy to pay for it, and co-create the experience with them, to confirm that you can deliver on your promises.

Over time, as you seek to enroll an ever-growing number of students, the tools, platforms, and strategies that you'll use to find them will grow in number of complexity. But to attract and enroll your pilot students, things are simpler. The specific tools, technologies, and messages that you'll use may vary depending on the industry that you're in, and the resources and expertise that you bring to bear. But it will always boil down to reaching out to people you already have some sort of connection with, either personally or professionally, and telling them about it.

Yes, that's right. Your first customers should be people you are already connected with. Not strangers on the internet who discover you through ads, blogs, partner referrals, social media, or some other happy accident of browsing the web. There are several reasons for this:

1. **They already like and trust you.** Selling anything can be difficult, and selling something for the first time can be especially challenging, because you probably haven't quite figured out what the most compelling parts are of your promise, or nailed the best way of presenting it. Given all that, it makes sense to start with an audience that is friendly, and at least somewhat on your side.

2. **You already have access to them.** This is very

important; you're already going to have to step out of your comfort zone to do this, but why make things harder than they have to be? The broad topic that you chose for your pilot course is of interest to people that you already have access to, isn't it? If so, then this is by far the easiest way of getting started. And if not, well, go back and revisit the section about choosing a pilot topic!

Of course, your personal and professional networks aren't an eternally renewable resource; you can't keep going back to find more and more customers, and special care must be taken to preserve the relationships that you've worked so hard to build. Hence the need for a carefully crafted process.

The first step is to make a list of the people you know who are likely to be interested in the subject matter that you're looking to teach, and more specifically in the outcome that you intend to deliver for them. This isn't about cold calling everyone you've ever met; the only people you should even approach with this are the ones who you think could very plausibly find it interesting.

And that approach is gentle, and soft. Remember, this is a co-creation process, so you aren't going to call them up and try to hard-sell them on paying for your pilot course, like some used car salesman! Rather, start by reaching out (through whatever channel is most comfortable for you, whether that means email, Facebook, text message, phone, or something else), and sharing that you're starting to work on a new project, and you'd love to run it by them and get their perspective, so could they make the time for a quick phone call sometime in the next couple of weeks. You might worry that people will be busy, or uncomfortable accepting a call, but my experience is that usually, people are surprised by how well this works, and how quickly.

It works because it's actually a pretty innocuous request. If you reach out to a few dozen people, you're likely to be on the phone with many of them in short order. On that call, you'll simply share the honest truth, which is that you're thinking about teaching a course about your chosen subject matter. Based on whatever background your contacts have that led you to believe they might be interested, you wanted to reach out and get their input – does this sound like a course that someone might be interested in signing up for? Is it, perhaps, a course that they themselves might like to sign up for?

The beauty of this question is that at this stage, it is purely hypothetical. If it isn't at all appealing to them, they can say "no", which is a gift to you because it means you'll have learned early that the market might not want this course quite as much as you thought. If that's what they say, ask them to elaborate on their reasons, emphasizing that you aren't trying to change their minds, but rather just want to understand; after all, you'd hate to go ahead with this plan if there isn't a demand for it!

But most people won't say "no" so soon in the conversation, if only because they want to be polite. This is a good thing, because even if they tell you they're not interested later, you want that decision to be as well informed as possible, so you can learn from it. Which brings us to the other possible answer that they can give you, which is "maybe". That's as good as it gets at this stage, because you haven't really given them enough information to make any stronger of a commitment. So if they do say "maybe", you can share more information about your pilot course, including what you plan on teaching, what the outcomes will be, when you're going to start, what a full priced course might eventually cost, whether you intend to offer a discount to your pilot students in exchange for their feedback through the process, and when the pilot is going to start. Having shared all that, you're now ready to ask the pivotal question: "would you like a spot in the pilot?"

There are now three possible answers to this question. The best answer for you, of course, is a "yes" – in which case you can arrange payment logistics, and you're off to the races. The next best answer is a "no"; you haven't enrolled a student, but you've still got a clear decision. Just as before, you'll want to press for more details as to why, emphasizing that you aren't trying to convince them, just to understand. The worst answer you can get is some variation of "maybe" ("I might", "I'm not sure", "I have to talk to my spouse", etc.). In that case, just ask for them to arrive at a decision one way or the other by a certain date (e.g. "next Friday"), so that you know where you stand. And if they don't make a decision by that time, you can treat it as a "no". Remember that the goal here isn't to aggressively push for a sale, but rather for you to gain clarity as to why they are or aren't interested.

If your pilot idea doesn't have legs, then a couple dozen calls is all that you'll have invested before learning that, and being able to pivot to a new idea that stands to be more valuable for others, and more lucrative for you. And if it does have legs, then a couple dozen phone calls should be all that it takes to fill your inaugural class with paying students. Now, again, I'll emphasize that the goal here isn't to enroll hundreds of students. Thanks to fat tail economics, and depending on the price you're charging for the pilot, anywhere from a handful to a few dozen is plenty. So suspend disbelief, step into your Zone of Proximal Development, and try it – if you're like many of my students, you'll find that the process is easier, more effective, and maybe even more fun than you're expecting.

Delivering Your Pilot:
Evolving Your Curriculum in Real-Time

Let's return for a moment to our story about the flight from New York to Chicago. However you pass the time on the flight, there's no question in your mind that the plane will in fact land in Chicago, within a small margin of error of the initial promised landing time. You'd never worry about the plane ending up in Minneapolis, Nashville, or anywhere else that isn't the destination on your ticket.

In fact, I'll bet that if at some point during the flight, the captain were to announce that you're heading in the wrong direction, you'd be surprised, and maybe even shocked or worried. But here's the really shocking part: even though the captain doesn't make those announcements, the plane is heading in the wrong direction for over 90% of the flight. You know how the in-flight channel with the map that shows your progress makes it look like you're flying in a straight line? Well, it's actually very zig-zagged, with constant little adjustments. The captain never bothers to mention it because it happens hundreds of times along the way, and it's totally normal; course corrections to adjust for variances in air pressure, new information about flight traffic, or the changing weight of the plane as fuel is consumed are all just normal parts of getting from point A to point B.

Now, other than giving you something to think about the next time you get on a plane, what does this have to do with online education or building courses? Just as with flying a plane to the destination you want to reach, the key to creating an excellent (and profitable) educational experience is having a lot of checkpoints along the way that tell you whether you're on track, and if not, allow you to course correct (no pun intended). That way, you're dramatically more likely to arrive at an end product that will truly support your students to achieve their success.

In earlier sections of this book, we explored some of the ways in which the delivery of education can evolve based on the new possibilities facilitated by new technologies and a good imagination. It's exciting, but can also be intimidating to the first-time course creator. The good news, though, is that all these evolutions and adaptations aren't important in the pilot phase, even though they matter a great deal in the long-term lifecycle of your education business. In fact, you've already laid the critical ground work for delivering your pilot course by:

1. Committing to the Zone of Proximal Development,

2. Selecting a topic that is of interest to your students,

3. Narrowing it down to the minimum viable outcome that you can deliver that would be meaningful for them,

4. Creating a one-page pilot plan outlining what you'll teach, and

5. Enrolling eager students through direct conversations.

If you've done all those things, the actual delivery will be pretty simple and straight-forward; you'll connect with your students to deliver your first lesson, and check in with them to make sure they're getting the hang of it. Once they've got it, you'll repeat the process with the second lesson, and then the third, and so on, until you've worked your way through your one page outline. You may very well find that you need to modify that outline as you go, and that's perfectly fine – this is the part where investing more time and energy to make sure your students are happy and successful is absolutely worthwhile.

Many course creators approach this part of the process thinking that it's about the technology of delivery, or the handouts or worksheets or exercises, but none of that is true. In fact, you'll want to keep the technological complexity to an absolute minimum. Depending on the nature and subject matter of your pilot, and the number of students that you enroll, you can deliver your course through a simple video-conferencing technology like Skype or Zoom. You'll definitely want to deliver the material live, though – pre-recorded videos are not only unnecessary at this stage, they're also counter-productive, as you can't get real-time feedback from students who watch videos the way you can when you're delivering the training to them live. It might not be as pretty or polished as your finished course will one day be, precisely because it will be more raw, authentic, and geared to be adaptable to what your students need in the moment. That level of intimacy will create a powerful bond between you and your students, a great experience for them, and the best opportunities for you to see what's working and what isn't, so that you can evolve and adapt on the fly. If all your students are in your geographic region, you can even deliver the pilot in person. The more opportunities you have to see your students' faces and hear their questions as you work through the material, the better.

Delivering your pilot will be a whirlwind experience with its fair share of ups and downs. Expect it to be exhilarating at times, and challenging at others. As long as you plan for that to happen, schedule time in your calendar to deal with all the questions and complications that you don't yet see coming, remain open to evolving your curriculum in response to the reaction of your students, and keep their successful outcomes as your top priority, everything will be fine. Within a few weeks or months of starting, your pilot course will be done, and the time will have come to make an important decision: what should you do next?

After Your Pilot:
Deciding to Pivot, Iterate, or Scale

It's been a long and winding road, and you've finally made it to the other side! You've chosen the topic of your pilot, narrowed it down to a minimum viable outcome, and created your one page plan. You reached out to likely prospects and enrolled some of them into your pilot. And then the real work began, with the delivery of your ideas. The process was exciting and exhilarating, with both ups and downs. But now it's done. The pilot has been delivered, and it's time to take stock and decide what you should do next. There are three dimensions on which you'll want to evaluate the pilot:

1. **Student outcomes.** Before they signed up for the pilot, you made promises about the outcomes that your students could look forward to. How has that played out? Are your students happy, and satisfied? Are you proud to tell others about their outcomes?

2. **Financial performance.** Did you make as much money as you had hoped with the pilot? Was it financially successful beyond your wildest dreams? Did it just meet your expectations? Or was it a disappointment?

3. **Your experience.** At the end of the day, it's very important for you to enjoy your work. So did you enjoy the experience of delivering your pilot? Was it more fun than you ever expected? Was it stressful and frustrating?

Now, in evaluating your pilot, remember that your first attempt at anything is bound to be messy – that's exactly why we pilot rather than building out a full course from scratch. It stands to reason, then, that the results of your pilot on these three dimensions are likely to be mixed; not terrible, but not always amazing, either. And that's perfectly fine, because you don't want to evaluate the pilot based on how it went, but rather by how it would go the next time, informed by what you've learned.

In other words, knowing what you now do, how would it go if you did it again? Do you feel confident that the next time you deliver this training it will be a smashing success on all fronts? Do you have ideas about how to make it great, that still need to be validated? Or was the experience such that the biggest takeaway was to never, ever try that again (unlikely, but much better for you to learn that sooner rather than later!)?

The relatively rare worst-case scenario is that you will have learned that this is not the path for you to take, your next step should be to pivot to a new idea. Go back to the drawing board, find a new topic and direction, and start over. And while you're at it, celebrate that it only took you a few months to learn this, rather than the years that it takes so many entrepreneurs!

Sometimes, you'll find that you have an idea of how to make it great, but you need to validate it to be sure. In that case, your next step is to deliver a second pilot course. Change everything that you think needs to be changed, validate your assumptions, and go from there.

And often, you will have learned enough from the pilot that you are now confident in your abilities to deliver an excellent course to a larger number of students. This is the ultimate win scenario, because now you're ready to move forward, and start building your education empire!

In Summary (TL;DR)

Let's quickly re-cap the most important points from this chapter (not including a Japanese concept that may in fact derail your course-building efforts; for that, you've got to read the actual chapter!):

- Business is risky, so it's understandable that we're inclined to de-risk the process, such as when business thought leaders encourage us to find our deep "why." But in practice, the search for this insight causes us to procrastinate.

- The search for deep meaning can only be successful when informed by real world experience. And the only way to know for sure what the market wants is to test by what is called a "pilot" course.

- To identify the topic for your pilot course, begin with the experiences you've had engaging with ideas and helping people. Look especially for the people you've helped in a way they truly appreciated. Identify broad, high-level topics. Then filter them through your expertise and access to a population who would value that topic.

- Then zero in on a narrow and specific topic, or the minimum viable version of your course. You can accomplish this by performing a thought exercise: if you had just over two hours long with your ideal prospect, what would you teach them that would transform their lives?

- The next step is to create a one-page outline of your course curriculum. List the big topics you need to cover; each of those is a lesson. Then under each topic, add a handful of bullets about the specific things you'll talk about. This outline is enough for you to sell your pilot course. It's also loose enough for you to be able to adjust, pivot, and iterate in real time, as you learn how to deliver your content in a way that best serves your students.

- When you co-create the course with your students, you're putting the IKEA effect into play. This says that people value a product more when they're involved in creating it. Your students become involved in the narrative of your course's creation, which sets you up for both short-term and long-term success.

- In this process, you'll enroll paying students into your pilot course and get paid before you've even built it. The exact mechanics of selling your pilot depends on many things, including the size of your audience, your advertising budget, etc. But the general idea is the same for all: reach out to those in your social and professional circles who potentially may be interested, and tell them about it. Whether they say "yes," "no," or "maybe" is useful information for you.

- When it's time to deliver your pilot, stick to the lowest possible technological complexity. The most important thing that will allow you to support your students and evolve through your delivery is your presence and hard work. You're also best off sticking to live delivery, where you see your students' faces and hear their questions as you work through the material.

- Recognize that the process may be bumpy and messy, but it's all part of your journey as an educator entrepreneur.

- Once you've delivered your pilot, you will evaluate your results on three dimensions: (1) what were the outcomes of your students, (2) how did the pilot perform financially, and (3) what was your experience delivering it.

- Based on those three criteria, you'll decide whether your next step should be to pivot to a new idea, iterate on your existing idea, or scale it up to reach more people.

Case in Point:
Megan Ayrault's Bodywork for Animals

Megan Ayrault, who has been teaching people, in-person and online, how to do body work for dogs and horses, isn't new to building online courses. But in the past, she worked on her own. After building up a list of about 2,000 subscribers, she would guess at what they wanted, present her courses, and hope they would like them. She made little progress and felt discouraged.

Then she discovered the process of co-creation, and her business was transformed. She enjoyed the process, especially the increased engagement with her audience. Getting feedback from her pilot students has also helped her create better courses than she did previously. Now she knows exactly what her students want, what questions they have, and where they trip up.

She made just over $2,000 from that first pilot. A few months later, she launched two more full online courses, quickly making additional income even without growing her subscriber list or audience. The increased interaction with her students and prospective students has also enriched her business in unexpected ways.

When doing the research for her first pilot course, for example, she came up with more course topic ideas than she would have thought of on her own. She also discovered a new market she hadn't considered before: aspiring professional body workers for animals – so she decided to pilot a course for them.

Today Megan offers several online courses in her Power of Touch for Animals E-Learning Center. "I have far better courses ready and presented better and my ability to communicate what I have to my market has improved," Megan says proudly.

She now thinks of her business as a "collaboration" with her audience. They tell her what they want and need to learn, and she creates programs for them.

"I feel reinvigorated to put energy into my business because of that collaboration with them. It's a totally different energy than working by myself," Megan says.

Onward,
To Your Education Empire!

"Our deepest fear is not that we are inadequate. Our deepest fear is that we are powerful beyond measure. It is our light not our darkness that most frightens us. We ask ourselves, who am I to be brilliant, gorgeous, talented and fabulous? Actually, who are you not to be?"

-Marianne Williamson

The bugaboo of almost every aspiring online entrepreneur is marketing. It is an enigma, at the same time Pandora's Box that threatens to turn us into slimy salesmen if deciphered, or else the Achilles heel that will be our downfall if we don't. We see the multi-million dollar launches of the marketers that we met earlier in this book, and at the same time wish we could do the same, and pray to never become like them. The beautiful irony, though, is that the more success you experience, the less marketing actually matters.

When you first introduce a new offer to the market – whether it be a course, or anything else – marketing is critical, because it's the only way for anyone to learn about what you offer. Since the offer is new, a prospect searching online or asking friends if they've heard of it will find nothing. Not only that, but the first version of anything is likely to see a great deal of improvement before reaching its final form – which again reinforces the need for good marketing. That's why, as you get started with your first forays into the Teach and Grow Rich opportunity with your first few pilot courses, you need every advantage you can find. This is why you learned in the last section to lean on the people who already like you and trust you, and harness the unfair advantage of the IKEA Effect.

But after you've delivered a pilot course or two, the tables begin to turn. Now you have more than promises to offer prospective students – you also have the proof of the results your past students have experienced. And because you opted to start with a small group of students and work with them to evolve your curriculum on the fly, you should have meaningful successes to point to. There are myriad options for continued growth at this point; you could grow an audience and following, invest in advertising budgets and marketing funnels, develop a network of joint venture partners, or any number of other things. The landscape of possible strategies and techniques is broad and rapidly changing, and which fits you best will depend on your industry, background, resources, and strengths. But ultimately, you'll need to make the case that your course is a great one to strangers, including your future students, evangelists, and partners. That will be made easier by the successful track record that following this process has created.

This opportunity is accessible to anyone in the world who has knowledge and expertise that can benefit those around us – and who in the world doesn't have something they could teach? It's a blue ocean of opportunity right now; despite massive abundance of information out there, there is very little real education of this nature, because we're just now beginning to understand what it takes to do it.

And unlike the California Gold Rush of 1848 and many of the opportunities that followed, the opportunity to Teach and Grow Rich won't follow the long tail distribution of a few hits taking the lion's share of the profits with everyone else left to pick up the scraps. Hundreds of millions of dollars will be made, and they will mostly be distributed in chunks of $50,000, $200,000, or a million dollars for the entrepreneurs who care to seize it. The numbers won't be attractive to Silicon Valley investors, but they're plenty attractive to most entrepreneurs seeking freedom and wealth. And most importantly, all that wealth will be earned by creating more real value and positive impact in the world than we've seen in a long time. So now, the only question is how large of an empire you are driven to create?

For some, a few annual enrollments of new students is more than enough to create both the impact and income that they care about. These are the lifestyle entrepreneurs, whose courses allow them the resources and freedom to set their own hours, travel, and invest their time and energy in the people, causes, and activities that they care about the most. They work for a year or two as others won't, developing and optimizing their course and marketing systems. And then they have a lifetime as most only dream – wealthy, free, and fulfilled.

For others, that first pilot course is just a small step on their journey as educator entrepreneurs. They aspire to serve hundreds, then thousands, then even more. Ultimately, it's about making a difference on a global level. They eventually hire coaches and advisors for their students, and grow an organization of dozens, or hundreds of people.

Both paths are great, important, and valid. Sometimes we

start on one, and find that we are called to pursue the other. Whichever path we take, we teach to grow rich, in the truest sense of the word. Rich because we've enriched the lives of others.

The future is long and bright, and begins with a single step: your first pilot course. So take that step, and with it your place in this movement of educator entrepreneurs.

Seminar on Advanced Course Marketing

My team and I periodically deliver free seminars on advanced course marketing where we share cutting-edge strategies and templates that you can use immediately:

Go here to see the schedule and register, for free:

http://mrse.co/seminar

To Go Far,
Go Together

An old African proverb tells us that "if you want to go fast, go alone, but if you want to go far, go together." I believe that wholeheartedly, because the book that you hold in your hands is the product of many, many people coming together in support of this vision.

At the top of that list is my wife Bhoomi, and our two children Priya and Micah. The process of writing a book is both highly solitary (sitting alone and writing), and highly communal (for development of ideas, and encouragement along the way). I got much of the latter from my wife, and having two young children I can safely say that without her, I would have had none of the former. And that support extends to my entire family, to whom I am so, so grateful.

As solitary as parts of the writing process can be, I was never alone in it, thanks to my incredible team at Mirasee, and especially Lexi Rodrigo, who assisted with the drafting of supplementary sections of this book, and Ashlee "Tree" Branch, who dug up the research that supported some of my crazier ideas.

Speaking of crazy ideas, I would never have found the inspiration and realization of the ideas in this book without the thousands of incredible community of course builders that I've worked with through our Course Builder's Laboratory. I couldn't be more proud of your hard work, commitment, and results.

I also had the privilege of in-depth conversations with a number of experts and pioneers in the emerging field of online education, including Matt Champagne, Dorie Clark, Matt Clark, Abe Crystal, Breanne Dyck, Ron Friedman, Gina Hiatt, Jim Hopkinson, Steve Kamb, James Maskell, Ankur Nagpal, Srikumar Rao, Stever Robbins, and Vanessa Van Edwards. I'm truly grateful for their insights.

All of the above brought the book to its raw form, and then the community of my students, colleagues, and friends came together as my "book insider's team" to read, review, edit, and provide feedback on how to make it truly great. There were too many of these to give them all credit here, but special thanks are due to Dolly Clarke, Jessica Eken, Emily Gillatt-Ball, Lisa Manyoky, Grazia Mariani, Kim Orr, Kathryn Potruff, Sarah Ravid, Paul Reimers, Valerie Utton, and Earl Williams. Odds are that if there's a section of this book that you especially liked, they had a hand in making it great. On the other hand, if there's something you particularly didn't like, the responsibility is probably all mine.

And even with all of that, many of the people reading this book would never have heard of it without the support of so many of our colleagues and partners who helped to get the word out.

To all of you, I am grateful. Thank you.

Appendix I:
The State of Online Courses

Every year, my company surveys its audience of service providers, independent professionals, and entrepreneurs, to gauge their interest and progress in course building. Below is a summary of the results for 2016 with 829 respondents, with comparison to the same data from the previous year. You will find the full report at http://mrse.co/state-of-online-courses.

Course Building Is On the Rise

It appears that respondents in 2015 who said they're considering online course creation are now creating their courses. In 2015, about 20% of respondents said they were in the process of creating their online courses. That percentage jumped to 35.6% this year.

A massive 93% of respondents have either pursued, are pursuing, or are interested in pursuing Course Building.

This is consistent with what we've been seeing in the industry lately. More vendors are offering platforms for independent online course creators (as opposed to academic or enterprise online educators).

And more than ever before, materials and programs about how to create and sell online courses are cropping up. There is growing interest in "edupreneurship," and the market is responding by providing the know-how and tools for online course creators.

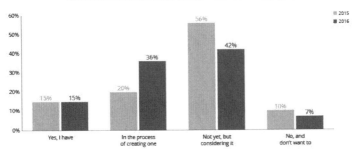

Impact and Income Are Primary Drivers

When asked what motivates them to create online courses, respondents most often said it was "to share my knowledge" and "to make money." Building an audience is the third most important goal respondents hope to achieve.

It's important for respondents to make a positive impact—to share knowledge and skills that help others. At the same time, they want to make money. This makes sense, because, unless they make money, they can't sustain their efforts to help others.

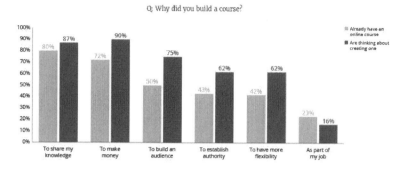

Desire to share their knowledge and make money is what is driving online course creators.

Q: Why did you build a course?

Reality Bites: Online Course Creators Aren't Reaching Their Goals

Respondents measure the success of their course mainly through the success and satisfaction of their students. This is consistent with 2015's findings, although more respondents in 2016 felt student success was most important.

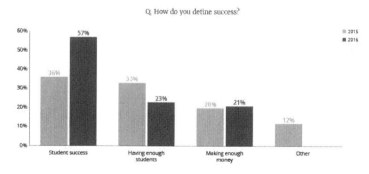

Success is measured mainly through the success and satisfaction of students.

Q: How do you define success?

Based on the above criteria, about 70% of the respondents considered their course to be at least somewhat of a success, while 11% said it was a failure:

**70% of online course creators deem their course
at least somewhat successful.**

Q: Do you consider your course a success?

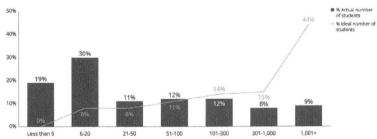

Part of the problem may be that they're not getting as many students as they hope to and at their ideal price point. While 44.4% of aspiring course creators hope to get over 1,000 students, only 8.9% of those who've sold courses have actually had this many students.

**Online course creators are falling short of their
ambitious student enrollment goals.**

Q: How many students do you hope will take your online course? How many students have taken your online course?

The vast majority of course creators are still getting no more than 50 students for their courses. A very small percentage have had more than 300 students. This picture is similar to last year's results. Online course creators are not meeting their expectations in terms of the number of students enrolling.

The story is consistent when it comes to pricing. About 73.7% of course creators want to charge upwards of $100, but in fact, only 47.3% do so. And a full 18.8% are giving away their courses for free.

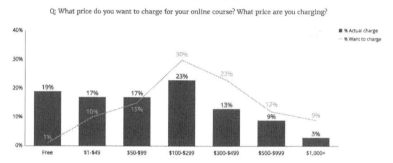

Online course creators are falling short of their course pricing goals.

Q: What price do you want to charge for your online course? What price are you charging?

Clearly, business owners get into online course creation hoping to reach many more people than they could by providing one-to-one services or coaching, as well as to earn a more passive income.

The reality of course creation, however, is that these hopes are not being met. Even though their courses may be effective, in the sense of helping students, they're neither getting enough students nor charging as much as they want to. So in terms of reach and income, many online courses are failing.

Course Creators Are Realizing
That Success Requires Marketing

Aspiring and current online course creators both recognize that marketing is one of the biggest challenges they must overcome. With almost 60% of online course creators enrolling fewer than 50 students, they recognize that their biggest impediment is marketing. They need help to fill those seats!

For those who are still considering creating online courses, time is the biggest impediment. But even this group who don't actually have a course to sell yet is already anxious over marketing. It even overtakes apprehension over technology, actual course creation, and other frustrations.

**Marketing their course is the biggest
challenge that course creators face.**

Q: What were/are the biggest impediments, challenges or frustrations in building your online course?

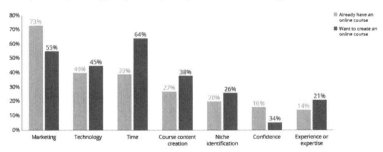

The Bottom Line

An increasing number of people are trying their hand at creating online courses, in the hopes of sharing their knowledge, making money, and widening their reach.

However, their expectations are not being met. They're not getting the number of students they expected to enroll, and they're not able to sell at their ideal price point. They want help to market their courses, use the technology involved, and make time for course building in their busy lives. Whether the industry is able to meet their needs remains to be seen.

Appendix II:
Gallery of Unlikely Educators

Throughout this book, you've met a number of online course creators who've been applying the co-creation process I've described. While reading through those illustrative case studies, you may have thought that they're special, just plain lucky, or have some kind of unusual abilities. Or you may have thought that you're the one whose circumstance, niche, or expertise is so special that no blueprint could possibly work for you.

We've compiled the profiles of other online course creators to show you that the Teach and Grow Rich opportunity is truly for anyone with valuable knowledge. To learn more about the individuals below and meet even more course creators, visit http://mrse.co/gallery.

∞ ∞ ∞

Joanna Armstrong:
Personal Transformation Coach through EFT

Joanna helps people transform from the person they are to the person they'd rather be, with the help of EFT Tapping.

Before becoming an online course creator, she had been helping one-to-one clients for seven years in a regular structured client-base business. Based on the wonderful online classes she attended herself, she thought maybe she could reach and help even more clients through the internet.

Joanna enrolled in Mirasee's Course Builder's Laboratory and was pleasantly surprised that she was able to get started right away and launch her first pilot course in just five weeks. Having struggled on her own previously, she thought the experience was "like magic."

"I definitely see that this is a very nice way of running a business, helping people getting results both for me, in my business so I can keep helping people, but also of course for my clients," Joanna says of her initiation into online courses. "They're getting great results. And because it's on the internet, because I provide a group forum where they can interact, we all help each other."

"I just want to create more courses," Joanna says.

∞ ∞ ∞

Autumn Birt:
Self-Published Author of Fantasy Fiction Books

Before becoming an online course creator, Autumn had self-published nine fantasy fiction books, all while holding a day job and caring for a family. She wrote four of those books in just one year.

After learning how to market her books, she transitioned from making $100 per year to $1,000 per month in books sales. Although it was a significant jump, it still wasn't enough for her to become a full-time entrepreneur. And that's what she realized: she didn't want to be just an author; she wanted to be an entrepreneur.

She put together a two-year plan to eventually teach a course about writing fantasy books, something she was an expert in and that wasn't widely available. She originally thought that creating an online course would be a slog. But upon learning about the co-creation process, she challenged herself to launch her first course in 60 days.

Aside from shortening her timeline, Autumn also ended up changing the focus of her course. "I had thought I was going to do one thing, but the marketing research said, 'Hey, this is a really good niche to launch your course for,'" Autumn recalls.

She says running her pilot was a lot of work, but in the end, she discovered "that I could actually run a successful course and I could teach." What's more, she has a waiting list of authors who want to take her course, and a clear strategy for marketing it in the lead-up to the annual National Novel Month.

∞ ∞ ∞

Diane Bolden:
Executive Coach, Leadership Development and
Organization Effectiveness Consultant, and Author
of *The Pinocchio Principle, Becoming a Real Leader*

Diane works one-on-one with business professionals who feel like work is sucking the life out of them and are ready to make a bigger impact doing meaningful work that inspires them.

Before becoming an online course creator, she was reaching a limited number of people. Plus, she had many ideas that she wasn't executing on fully: she had written a book, *The Pinocchio Principle*, but gave away more copies than she sold. She also developed several programs but never properly launched them.

She decided to finally get serious and launch an online course to complement her book. "I've always wanted to have a course that would allow people to go deeper into the concepts and give them more of an experience that would be transformational," Diane said.

Diane previously built products based on assumptions she had about her audience, and then she would second-guess herself and question what she made. But with the co-creation process, she discovered what issues and problems her audience was struggling with, and how to frame her course "in such a way that it would really help them solve a problem they haven't been able to solve before."

After being coached through becoming an online course creator, Diane is inspired to provide the same level of support to her own students, "because I've experienced the power of that," Diane says, "It is truly exceptional."

∞ ∞ ∞

Kelly Bonanno:
Organic Beauty and Wellness Blogger
at *Savvy Beauty Scene*

Kelly left her TV network job to raise her kids, which got her started blogging and working part-time to promote an organic products company. She's passionate about helping women detoxify their lifestyle and environment so they can enjoy better health.

Kelly became interested in online courses as a way to reach more people and educate them in a more intimate and hands-on way than with blog posts, other written material, or even in-person presentations.

As she started working on her course about organic living, Kelly realized that she had enough information for two separate courses. She broke down her initial idea for a massive course into two online courses.

Kelly suspected that her course idea was something that people didn't even know they wanted until they had experienced it. And so she spent plenty of time doing market research to validate that people wanted the course enough to pay for it.

Once she got that validation, she launched her pilot course and enjoyed it tremendously. "I'm in my wheelhouse doing this," she recalls "It was great. And the feedback I got was phenomenal."

Some of the feedback included suggestions for Kelly to start a podcast, along with other great ideas for her business, which she's now working on.

∞ ∞ ∞

Chris Brooks:
eCommerce Trainer for Artists and Artisans

Chris runs a business helping artists and artisans create and market their products through online stores. He used to give in-person courses, which he found difficult. "There were so much logistics involved and I had to charge so much," Chris says. He also found the number of people he could reach to be extremely limited.

By doing market research, Chris was able to identify what his target audience struggled with and planned a pilot course around that. He was both excited and anxious about the prospect of getting paid while testing his idea for his course. He was nervous about getting people to buy his pilot course, but he felt exhilarated when they did.

Some of his students' results were phenomenal. One got top rankings on Google within the first month; another got a ton of publicity and traffic. "It increased my confidence and it really made me believe in not only myself, but my students, the process and the course itself," Chris says.

∞ ∞ ∞

Patrick Ching:
Nature Artist and Art Teacher

Before becoming an online course creator, Patrick was teaching art classes to groups of 3-4 people. For 10 years, he had been wanting to bring his classes online so that he could teach more people.

Finally, he committed to learning how to become an online course creator and promised himself he would do whatever it took to launch his first course.

The idea of co-creating his course and starting with a pilot course first were new to him. He appreciated learning how to approach his potential students to find out what they wanted to learn from him.

For his four-week pilot course, Patrick taught his students a complex painting. Nevertheless, he says, "they have amazing results to show for it and I'm sure they're going to be very happy to do testimonials for me when it's time to expand my online classes."

The results opened his eyes. "I ran into some things I didn't expect," Patrick shares, "I definitely know the next time what kind of things I can look for and what kind of things I can improve on."

∞ ∞ ∞

Karen Chovan:
Principal, Enviro Integration Strategies

Karen works with managers of projects and change initiatives to help them integrate the environmental, social, and economic aspects of their work to have beneficial outcomes.

She became interested in online courses because she wanted to take her message to a broader audience and have a greater impact. She felt excited at the prospect of not just going project by project, but also having the ability to influence how a larger number of people do projects.

When she learned the co-creation process, one of her biggest revelations was the need to focus on a specific niche, understand her target audience, and speak to them in their language. She says she found it enlightening to "find a way to provide a solution to their challenges and have some results for them."

∞ ∞ ∞

Dorie Clark:
Marketing Strategist, Author of *Reinventing You* and *Stand Out,* and Instructor at the Fuqua School of Business at Duke University

Dorie previously experimented with creating online courses for other entities, but she held back from creating her own because she was worried about whether there was enough demand for her course idea. She didn't want to waste precious time creating something the marketplace didn't want.

By following the co-creation process, she discovered that her audience was interested in a course on how to become a recognized expert. She dove into both the quantitative and the qualitative responses to her survey and used what she learned, not only to come up with an in-demand course topic, but also write a sales page that appealed to her prospects.

Dorie worried that no one would sign up for her pilot, but 45 minutes after emailing her list about it, "I was astonished because I had hundreds of emails and it turned out that I had to immediately go in and shut off the purchasing mechanism because we had already sold out the slots on the pilot."

"In about 45 minutes, I ended up taking in about $23,500 and I had far more people than that emailing me, asking if they could somehow be in the course," she adds, "And I was in the sad, but fortunate position of having to turn them away."

Dorie has since completed her pilot and launched her full course.

∞ ∞ ∞

Maggie Cowan-Hughes:
Instructor, Buteyko Method of Breathing

Maggie helps people manage asthma and sleep problems through the Buteyko Method breathing technique. She began by teaching people on Skype and eventually got the idea to create an online course.

On her own, Maggie spent five months creating her masterpiece of a course. Then she launched it to 100 people, along with an offer for a free introduction. Few people signed up for the freebie and nobody bought her course.

But this did not discourage Maggie. She's on a mission to spread the word about the Buteyko Method. She knows it works and she feels her work is important. "It's so amazing when somebody says, 'I'm not snoring anymore,' or 'I don't need my medication anymore after many years of being dependent on medication,'" Maggie declares.

Instead of quitting, she learned how to create and sell online courses the right way.

The idea of the pilot as a trial empowered her. "The idea that it didn't have to be perfect took a whole lot of the pressure off what I was doing," Maggie says. "And suddenly the whole thing became exciting."

Even though she didn't know how to sell, when she offered her pilot course to 70 people, 7 of them enrolled in her course. In doing so, she achieved her two goals:

proving that she could teach Buteyko breathing online, and getting testimonials from happy students.

∞ ∞ ∞

Mandi Ellefson:
Helping Service Businesses Scale in Less Time

Mandi helps established service businesses like marketing services, agencies, and software services to scale up. She was working with clients one-on-one, but wanted to have a group program as well.

Her first attempt to launch a product, following advice from internet marketing "experts," was a bust. Even though her offering was great, she lost money on it. She didn't run the program; she didn't have enough sales to make it worth her time.

Next time around, Mandi followed the co-creation process. The research made a big difference. She discovered that her prospects were keen on a topic she had been avoiding.

Mandi ended up piloting her course by accident. She had an opportunity to address a friend's audience, so she offered her pilot just to see what would happen. Two people signed up. Then, just from having conversations with other people, more folks enrolled. The pilot financed the development of her full course.

"And now, it's a lot easier for me to work with that [larger] number of people and work a lot less," Mandi says, "In fact, this year, I'm looking at cutting my work schedule down to 15 hours a week. There's no way I'd be able to do that [before]."

∞ ∞ ∞

John Ford:
Workplace Mediation Expert, Founder of the
HR Mediation Academy, and Author, *Peace at Work:
The HR Manager's Guide to Workplace Mediation*

John supports HR professional's worldwide to approach the inevitable workplace conflict they face with greater confidence and ease. "I wanted to have an online education company," John says, "but I didn't know how to make it happen. I was feeling stuck."

Originally, John wanted to create an online course focused on workplace mediation, to complement his book. But as he went through the research phase of the Course Builder's Laboratory, he discovered that his market wanted help with challenging workplace relationships. The shift was huge, John says, because he could have made a "fatal error." Instead, he sold out his pilot course with 12 people paying $197 each.

"I'm pretty confident in where I'm going. My dream of having an online company, focused on education that frees me geographically, to have more work-life balance, enjoy life without working too hard—I'm seeing that," he says, "It's getting closer to me by the day."

∞ ∞ ∞

Alana Fournet:
Functional Diagnostic Nutrition Practitioner
and Transformational Wellness Coach, Owner of the
Intentional Living Project, Focused on Optimal Health,
Financial Wealth, and Relationships

Alana runs a business called the Intentional Living Project, an online community wellness center focused on optimal health, financial wealth, and fulfilling relationships.

She started out with so many ideas of what she wanted to bring to the world, but she was all over the place and never got any of them off the ground.

Doing market research for her pilot course helped her to focus her efforts by first listening to what her market was saying that they needed and wanted. By digging into the market analysis, she was able to narrow down the focus of her offer.

Alana has successfully launched her pilot and received feedback from her participants. The experience also gave her clarity about which format of online courses she enjoys the most and brings the desired transformation to her students.

"This process has really helped me to identify where I want

to be in the world of health or wellness, to really identify my niche, and know who it is that I love working with," Alana says.

∞ ∞ ∞

Steve Gordon:
Business Consultant to Professional Service Firms,
Founder of Clients on Autopilot System™,
Publisher of *The Unstoppable CEO* blog, and Author
of *Unstoppable Referrals: 10x Referrals Half the Effort*

Business was good, but Steve and his team wanted to help more people and scale what they were doing. That's why they looked at launching an online course. But when they tried launching courses in the past, they had little success.

Until they discovered the co-creation process.

They learned how to do deep market research before putting the course together. Instead of spending weeks building a course, they tested their idea by taking it through the pilot process. "We made some money upfront before we created it which was really nice," Steve recalls, "And it helped us get off on the right foot."

One year after completing the Course Builder's Laboratory, Steve saw a definite growth in his business. They've already sold tens of thousands of dollars' worth of their course. But more importantly, the course has been a good way for them to bring in high-end clients and qualify them as they go through our course.

Many of their students eventually decide to hire them. He observes, "We had people coming in and buying our course, and then at the end of that they said, 'You know, this was really great. We're really happy with this, but will you do this for us? Will you work with us one on one?'"

∞ ∞ ∞

Edward Haskins:
Accountability Coach and Owner of Accountability Sensei

Edward is an entrepreneur and business coach with 20 years of experience. As an accountability coach, he helps entrepreneurs transform into high-performance entrepreneurs.

After reading the first edition of *Teach and Grow Rich* and watching one of Mirasee's webinars, Edward ran away with the idea and launched a pilot course by himself.

He validated his idea by posting on his personal Facebook account, asking his business contacts if the topic was something they'd be interested in. After receiving positive feedback, He went ahead and outlined a five-week pilot program.

To sell the pilot, he put together a video sales letter (VSL) script on Google Docs and shared the link to his Facebook contacts. The result: he sold a total of 30 seats in his pilot course (his target was 25), each paying $595! He didn't even produce the actual VSL yet.

The entire process was quick and, for experienced entrepreneurs, unrefined. But Edward says, "Who needs fancy funnels when you're just validating your idea?"

∞ ∞ ∞

Ryan Hurd:
Stay-at-Home Dad, Dream Researcher, Educator,
and Author of *Dreamstudies.org*

Ryan runs *Dreamstudies.org*, a blog about dreams, consciousness studies, and imagination studies. As a stay-at-home Dad, Ryan's been struggling to earn an income by publishing multimedia eBook products. He was putting a lot of time and energy creating them without knowing the outcome.

"How can I have the biggest impact in the least amount of time?," he wondered.

Despite his experience running online courses for other institutions, he found the Course Builder's Laboratory "revolutionary."

Not only did he learn to pitch and sell an idea, he also learned to be comfortable with charging more money. Since he used to sell eBook kits for $5 to $20, he found it a big leap to ask for 10 times that amount.

When he did launch his pilot, Ryan ran into a happy problem. His course sold out in less than eight hours, and many more members of his audience wanted to get in. He put them on a special call-first list for his second pilot. When he opened that up, his conversion rate was 30 percent.

He was pleasantly surprised that he got those results without deceitful, manipulative, or cheesy marketing. He discovered that marketing "is about reaching out to people and finding what they care about and then providing that."

"I'm realizing that teaching a course is easily integrated into my life," Ryan says, "I'm delighted that I found a new income stream that's not only fun but is reliable."

∞ ∞ ∞

**Dr. Lise Janelle:
Former Chiropractor, Heart-Centered Success Coach,
Founder of the Centre for Heart Living**

As a heart-centered success coach, Lise helps people live from their hearts so they can live extraordinary lives. To make a bigger impact, she decided to create group online programs.

Piloting, Lise says, "was like being a mad scientist and observing what was happening, seeing the results, what people like, what they didn't like, how people were reacting to it to give us ideas on how we could create a solid program afterwards."

Lise has since scaled to a six-month course.

This course-building process has given Lise confidence.

"And confidence is half the equation. When you feel you know what you are doing, it's a lot easier to have clarity on the next steps to be able to get up, to pull the team together, and to work together, and to have fun," Lise says.

∞ ∞ ∞

Melissa Josue:
Blogger at *Happyhealthyrelationship.com* **and Dating**
Coach for Women

Melissa had a full-time job and, on the side, was blogging and coaching women who were dating single dads or recently-divorced men, when she discovered the Course Builder's Laboratory.

She had tried launching online courses on her own in the past, but her results were only "okay." Her main goal was to be able to stop offering one-on-one coaching, especially since she was pregnant at the time and would be busy with a newborn baby.

When she launched her pilot while on maternity leave, she sold five spots at $197–nothing spectacular, but "that's the most that I have made at one time in my business," Melissa says. That validated that her audience was willing to pay for the content in her pilot class.

At the same time, she was able to interact with her pilot students and really get to know their struggles. She also learned what they needed in the course, including the way of delivery they preferred. She also discovered what modes of delivery she found most enjoyable and energizing.

Most important of all, Melissa says, she learned "what kind of business I really want, how do I want to show up in the world through this work that I'm doing."

∞ ∞ ∞

Greg Lee:
Natural Treatments and Remedies for People with Persistent Lyme disease

As founder of the Two Frogs Healing Center, Greg helps patients recover from persistent Lyme disease through natural treatments and remedies. For the past five years, he's also been giving in-person training for doctors, chiropractors, acupuncturists, and herbalists. He wanted to offer an online version of the course for people who can't make it to the face-to-face training.

But he had misgivings about delivering content online, especially when he felt the online courses he took himself weren't all that engaging.

And so he found the process of piloting and co-creating his course to be incredibly useful. He could get his participants' feedback and create a course that met their needs.

He has taken that feedback and launched his full course. It sold out in four days. He now has a waiting list for when his course opens again.

Greg now plans to develop his own online training university. Online course creation is "for people who really feel they have a message," Greg says, "They have information they really want to help other people with."

∞ ∞ ∞

Maria Liu:
Licensed Psychotherapist and Love Success Mentor

Maria helps smart, successful, independent women find true love fast through her company, Love Success Formula. She had been working privately with clients when she got the idea to turn her love success formula into an online product that they could consume at their own pace and in the comfort in their own homes.

The experience of her pilot course drove home for Maria the importance of trialing before launching a full course. She thought she only needed six weeks to deliver 20 video lessons. It turned out, she needed four months.

She found her pilot students to be very forgiving about the extended timeline. "'Maria,' they told me, this is a pilot, you know, this is what a pilot is for, to find out what needs to be changed and improved before you do the actual launch,'" she recalls.

"The moment I clicked the send button to my students for the first time sending them my very first welcome video was an amazing, exhilarating experience," Maria says. "I feel so grateful that I get to deliver my life's work through an online course format."

∞ ∞ ∞

Nathan Lively:
Sound Engineer and Career Coach and Trainer to Sound Engineers

Nathan is an experienced sound engineer who provides career coaching and technical training to other sound engineers.

Before becoming an online course creator, he struggled to find enough clients. He would offer what he thought were excellent services, but few people would buy. He knew he had to figure out how to make products people wanted, not what he thought they wanted.

He threw himself into market research. Aside from surveying his audience, he had conversations with 12 people who responded to his survey. This allowed him to "get ideas from them about what people would buy, what courses would be most popular, and the kind of marketing language I would need to sell it to them," Nathan says.

He discovered that the majority of his audience wanted technical training, so he built a pilot course around that. Skeptical of the process at first, Nathan was pleasantly surprised with his results: 22 seats sold.

He plans to use the piloting process to quickly test for

product-market fit before investing heavily in developing any single program.

"I was surprised that it worked as well as it did," he says.

∞ ∞ ∞

Stephanie Losi:
Software Developer, IT Risk Management Expert,
and Former Journalist

After working for seven years in risk management, Stephanie got tired of saying "no" to people all the time and wanted to say "yes" for a change. She began working on a Udemy course, then she realized she had no idea how to market her course, or even how to give her students what they needed.

She appreciates how the piloting process helps her keep improving her courses. She loves hearing from her students. "It's like a rising tide with all the boats, [where] feedback from one person ends up helping a thousand," Stephanie says.

Today Stephanie has several courses on Udemy. "My next thing is just to create a lot more courses in areas where I feel there are gaps and where student's concerns haven't really been addressed yet," she says, "I'll just keep making courses in this area if it's something that people are really responding to and needing."

∞ ∞ ∞

Kristin Lund:
Former Lawyer, Mediator, Facilitator, and Conflict Resolution Trainer, and Partner at Winding Path, Inc.

As an experiential educator, the idea of putting information out without engaging people didn't jive with Kristin. She wanted, not just to inform, but to educate others.

Kristine's goal was to enrol 15 students in her pilot course. She sold out in two weeks, and those who missed out passionately wanted to get into the course. "Someone came to my house with an envelope full of cash and insisted that I had to add her to the course," Kristine recalls. "So I ended up having 17."

Becoming an online course creator has expanded Kristin's horizons. Coming from a city with a population of 145,000 "teaches you to think a bit small," she says. But teaching an online course, has "expanded my thoughts in terms of what this business could be."

When she started, she thought it would just be a side business. Now, Kristine thinks "It doesn't have to be limited to 30 percent of my income and in fact, you know, it could be something that I could really grow."

∞ ∞ ∞

Molly Mahoney:
Voice and Business Teacher to Performers

When Molly joined the Course Builder's Laboratory, she had already started working on an online course teaching performers how to manage their careers like a business.

Because of this, she didn't go through the entire validation process taught in Course Builder's Laboratory. She launched her pilot... and it failed. While she was able to sell her pilot, when she sold it for a higher price as a full course, nobody wanted to buy it.

Nevertheless, Molly says, it was "the most magical thing that could have happened for my business." The experience made her pivot and launch a course about Facebook Live within a week. Since beginning the program, Molly has earned over $50,000.

Her biggest discovery: "There're so many ways that you can go with the information that you have and how you're going to teach it and who you're going to teach it to and being ready to make those little adjustments is where I think you find that true success."

∞ ∞ ∞

Ellen Martin:
Runs InfoTeam, a Digital Marketing,
Web Hosting and Web Design Company

Ellen wanted to transition her business from providing web hosting and design to doing more training. However, she felt she didn't have time to learn how to be an online course creator and, besides, most programs she bought in the past ended up sitting on the shelf, unused.

Although time was a challenge for Ellen, she followed through and launched her first course. What made a difference was receiving individual support from her coach and encouragement from a mastermind group of other course creators.

"I was able to take that passion of teaching, combine it with my love for technology and create a course that teaches people how to overcome their terror of the tech and be able to move forward with their own online courses," Ellen says.

∞ ∞ ∞

Cherry Menlove:
Blogger on Lifestyle and Homemaking,
and Author of *Cherry Menlove's Unique Party Ideas,*
Cherry Menlove's Easy Parties, Cherry Menlove
The Handmade Home, **and** *The Little Book of Peace*

Cherry was a successful lifestyle blogger and author of several books before becoming an online course creator. Nevertheless, she began her journey at a tumultuous time in her life: having twins, a life-threatening disease in the family, and even legal troubles.

But she forged ahead and launched her pilot course. "I remember walking the dog with my family and I kept getting these little notifications on my phone that I had another sale, another sale, another sale," Cherry recalls. The total sales from her pilot was £1,600.

But the benefits of the pilot went beyond financial. "You learn such an enormous amount about yourself, about potential students, about the material, about the topic, about the delivery, about working with a coach, about the technical aspect of it," she says.

Now Cherry is about to launch her full course and is using the pilot methodology to write her fifth book.

∞ ∞ ∞

Lizzie Merritt:
Work-at-Home Mom, Training Manager at Mirasee,
Helps Women Overcome Body Image Issues

Lizzie was a blogger with a tiny email list when she launched her pilot course. Although she had plenty of apprehensions, she was spurred on by her mission to show moms, in particular, that they can be happy right now, no matter what their size or shape.

Lizzie says the experience was terrifying but "completely worth it and wonderful." She cites three benefits to piloting. First, is the confidence she gained with being able to launch and sell an online course. The second benefit is earning an income from the pilot. And the third is being able to make changes to the course as she received feedback from her students.

Since becoming Mirasee's Training Manager, Lizzie has gotten too busy to work on her full course. Nevertheless, just the experience of proving she can build, launch, and sell an online course has been valuable to her. "You can't put a price on that," Lizzie says.

∞ ∞ ∞

Zaheen Nanji
Corporate Trainer, Professional Speaker,
Owner of a Wellness Center, and Author,
Attract Your Ideal Weight and *The Resilience Reflex*

As a paid speaker, Zaheen was traveling so much and spending too much time away from home. That's when she started looking into building online courses as another stream of income.

Yet Zaheen had a lot of misgivings about becoming an online course creator. She didn't have time, for one thing. Aside from speaking to groups, she also runs a wellness center with her spouse. She was also concerned about not having a big email list. "Who's going to want to take my course?" she wondered.

With discipline and hard work, she was able to launch her pilot course. She found it freeing not to have to create a "perfect" course before launching. "A pilot is meant to be there, that you can try things out with a small group of people, see how it works for everyone including myself and then come back to it, tweak it and then offer it again," Zaheen reflects.

Her advice for aspiring course creators: "Just take that first step."

∞ ∞ ∞

Cyndy Porter:
Image Consultant and Portrait Photographer Specializing in Women at Cyndy Porter Style & Photography

Cyndy's business was doing well, but she wanted to help more women all over the world to look and feel their best. That's when she started to look for a way to have a greater online presence.

She had been doing in-person workshops, so she knew what she wanted to teach in her online course. But when she piloted it with a target of 12 students, the demand astonished her. "I sent out one email, I got 17 women and one of them was across the world from Saudi Arabia," Cyndy recalls. "And so I was just really excited to find out that there seems to be a very big market for what I do and that it was a great way to test it."

She thought she would just break even with her pilot course, but she ended up making a profit.

"Now I am looking at the feedback that I got from the pilot, what worked and what didn't work and I'm in the process of creating my full-blown product which I think is going to be a huge success," Cyndy says.

∞ ∞ ∞

Paul Potter:
Teacher, Mentor, Physical Therapist, Author of *On Fire: Ignite Your Passion with a Cash Therapy Practice*, and Host of the *Functional Freedom* Podcast

Paul recently sold his physical therapy practice to focus full-time on coaching other entrepreneur therapists start their own successful practices.

He was ready to go into seclusion mode to work on his first online course. He learned how to do his research and pilot his idea instead. Paul had to overcome his fear of rejection, but in the end he did free coaching calls for 25 physical therapists. Those calls opened his eyes to what their problems were and what they wanted to learn.

Aside from getting a better understanding of his audience, Paul says those calls helped me build loyalty among his small audience.

Halfway through his launch, Paul said, "I can start to see in their minds, it's starting to click and then to see them take that and do acts of courage and step out into the unknown by virtue of our interaction has just been really, really, really rewarding."

∞ ∞ ∞

Kathryn Pottruff, MSPM, PMP:
Consultant, Workshop Facilitator,
and Coach in Project Management

Kathryn helps individuals and organizations improve the way they manage projects. She would travel all across Canada to address groups of 20-30 people. While she enjoyed the interaction and the impact she was making, she didn't like all the travelling.

So Kathryn decided to become an online course creator. At first, she resisted the idea of doing market research for her online course. "Nobody is going to tell me anything that I don't know already," she recalls. But she was in for an epiphany. "I thought I knew my students well, but not nearly as well as I knew them after I had done the research," she says. "I thought I understood, but now I really get it and that's made all the difference in the world."

Now that Kathryn has completed her pilot and is creating her full course, she says the experience has been "a journey of rediscovering my passion."

∞ ∞ ∞

Gary Simmons:
Martial Arts Teacher

As a martial arts teacher with a successful brick-and-mortar business for over 20 years, Gary wanted to reach more people. And so Gary tried creating online courses on his own. He would build them, put them online, and then wait for students to come. "It just didn't happen," Gary remembers.

Turns out, he still had plenty to learn. "I knew about searching keywords and doing the research," Gary remembers, but he discovered he needed "the structured way of researching and looking for the problem language and eavesdropping in on conversations online to really firstly ascertain if there is a need for the products and services as well as if it going to be a viable business."

Gary's goal is to have a thousand students around the world. "That would really set me up and take me, my finances, and the business to the next level," he says.

∞ ∞ ∞

Jerome Stone:
Registered Nurse, Speaker, and Author of *Minding the Bedside: Nursing from the Heart of the Awakened Mind*

Jerome is passionate about teaching people, especially nurses, about stress reduction and resilience through mindfulness and awareness. When he wrote his book, he expected things to work out like they did in the movie, Field of Dreams. But the readers didn't come. That's when Jerome realized he still had a lot to learn.

Even though he had a small list of less than 500 people, when he opened up his pilot course, he sold 16 seats.

He found it fascinating to be able to make real-time changes to the course based on his students' feedback. "I felt such a sense of success and so much pride in having done it," he recalls, "It gave me such confidence in really being able to then do additional courses, to really be able to serve people best."

Since then, Jerome has launched his first full online course and is working on another one.

∞ ∞ ∞

Kathleen Tozier:
Wellness Coach, Blogger at *KathleenTozier.com*,
Host of the *Indomitable Women* Podcast,
and Author of *Unleash Your Inner Magnificence*

Kathleen coaches women suffering high levels of chronic pain, depression, and anxiety. She left a 20-year career in medical transcription to fulfill her lifelong dream of helping women through a web-based business.

At first, she thought that would involve offering ebooks, workbooks, and other written materials. Then she discovered that "building a self-paced course became a wonderful idea because the clients are able in the off times and wee hours to go through materials at their own pace, watch videos and things of that nature that give them connection to me and communication with me, but don't always require my first-person presence," Kathleen says.

Since she works with women who deal with chronic pain, depression, anxiety, grief, and other sensitive issues, she found it challenging to design a course that wasn't as high-touch as one-on-one counselling. She came up with a middle ground that combined group calls, one-on-one sessions, and workbooks.

She piloted with six women, each paying $527. "Doing this high-touch, high-contact pilot was helping me clearly understand how I would structure something more permanent and gain the balance that was ideal for my particular target audience," Kathleen says.

∞ ∞ ∞

Edward Vilga:
Yoga Teacher, Visual Artist, Film Writer and Director,
and Author of Several Books Including *Yoga In Bed*
and *Downward Dog: A Novel*

Edward became interested in online courses, because he thought it would make an excellent component of his eighth book. He wanted to create "something that people would truly want to buy and use and transform their lives."

Learning the validation and co-creation process was transformative for Edward. "I am very much a member of the old-school creative world where I create my best work and I refine it and there's, you know, some development maybe with my agent or an editor. And then I put it out there and you more or less hope for the best," he says, "It confirmed that my ideas were valid, and it showed me what people responded most strongly to, and it allowed me to create something that I was super confident in on multiple levels."

It has also transformed the way he writes books. For his book proposal, for example, he spoke with 50 individuals, just to clarify his ideas.

Edward's market research was so effective at helping him craft an offer that, although he aimed to get 12 people into his pilot course, he ended up enrolling 42, "without even trying." "People were interested in the topic and the way that I've narrowed in on it," he says.

The experience has given him so much confidence. As he

iterates his full course, Edward says, "I know that it works. I know that I'm not just hoping for the best."

∞ ∞ ∞

Ryan Williams:
Business Consultant and Coach, Host of the *Stories from the Influencer Economy* Podcast, Author of *The Influencer Economy: How to Launch Your Idea, Share It with the World, and Thrive in the Digital Age*

Ryan has helped entrepreneurs and companies big and small share their ideas, products, and projects with the world. His clientele includes executives from Disney, Warner Bros, Activision, Microsoft, and Google. To establish himself as an expert in the digital age and new economy, Ryan wrote his book, *The Influencer Economy.*

Aside from that, the book helped Ryan build a community around his ideas. Soon they were telling him to create a course. But, Ryan thought, "How do I build it without too much risk and too much time? I don't want to waste time making a course no one's going to buy."

The course creation process turned out to be the answer. Ryan found that it didn't just help him create his course, it's also helping him update his book, improve his podcast, and grow his consulting business.

"The biggest surprise for the course is these bigger bonds that I'm forming with my students that I wasn't expecting, that don't come from just having a podcast or writing a book," Ryan says.

∞ ∞ ∞

Allen Wyatt:
Manages Content Websites Through
Sharon Parq Associates

After running successful websites for 20 years, Allen felt that his business has become stagnant. He wanted to venture into making video-based training content, and that got him looking at online courses.

From Danny, Allen learned how to inquire from his audience, get feedback from them, and get their help to create a product he would eventually offer them.

His pilot course was exceptionally successful. "I went to bed one night after a day and a half knowing that I would probably reach 75 people by the next day. And before I could get the spigot turned off and get the doors closed, I had 95 people who had signed up for the course at $95 per person," Allen recalls, "And this was a course that wasn't even completely finished yet. It was one that was still in development and they helped me to make that a final product."

Looking back, he says, "I should've started sooner but I'm glad that I finally did it."

Appendix III:
The Author's
Teach and Grow Rich Story

My Teach and Grow Rich story began in 2008 when I created the startup, MaestroReading. I wanted to change the world by building software that teaches children how to read. I raised money, hired people, built a prototype, and won awards and accolades for innovative business thinking.... but I didn't make any money.

While I had done well researching the problem of elementary reading and building something that would help kids to learn to read, it never occurred to me to ask parents or teachers what *they* wanted or needed to help their kids. And so, even though both kids and industry experts loved our software, the parents and teachers who would have been our customers never understood its value. And while we might have had a chance to recover, we were hit by the kidney punch that was the market crash of 2008. The result: my company was down for the count, having achieved nothing but saddling me with a quarter of a million dollars of debt. Even worse, while building MaestroReading, I had neglected my consulting practice. Not only did I have massive debt, I also had no source of income to start paying it.

So I did the only thing I felt I could do: rebuild my practice. It worked, and within a couple of years, I had built up to a lucrative business. The target market I could serve the best, and create the most value for was small business owners with fewer than 10 employees, businesses in the very early stage, who were just starting out. I found more than enough of them who could afford my services, and they were the bread and butter of my practice. However, I found even more businesses who needed a ton of help but couldn't afford one-on-one coaching with me.

That's when I hit on a "clever idea": I would build an online course to teach aspiring entrepreneurs everything they needed to know. I didn't see it then, but in hindsight, I was repeating the same mistake I made with MaestroReading. After (correctly) identifying a problem in the market, I didn't ask anyone if my proposed solution was something they wanted or needed. I assumed that I knew best, and so I rushed ahead to invest thousands of hours building a massive training course that I "knew" they needed. It was the "build it first" approach that 99% of entrepreneurs follow, and it almost always leads to failure. The training program (called "Marketing That Works"—oh, the irony!) was a flop. I've never done the math, but there's a good chance the dollars I made relative to the hours I spent on that project would make for the lowest wage I've earned in my lifetime.

Nonetheless, I'm grateful for that plot twist. The product never sold well, but trying to figure out how to sell it put me on the road to success. I started out like everybody else who sets out to build a business online: bouncing from one shiny strategy to another. I barely saw even a hint of success, until I stumbled onto guest posting in 2011. After my first couple of guest posts landed on major sites and drove substantial traffic back to my own blog, I realized this was a winning strategy and threw myself into it. In the first year, I had written over 80 guest posts for major blogs, in addition to posts for my own blog. This earned me the nickname "The Freddy Krueger of Blogging" (one reader commented, "It's like you're Freddy Krueger... wherever I turn, you're there!").

I wasn't making much money from my online marketing course, but what I did sell came from those who had discovered my work online, followed my ideas, and subscribed to my email list. So, I set out to grow my audience in the most strategic and intentional way I could. And because I was focused on building my audience, as opposed to selling a product or service, it was natural for me to concentrate on what they wanted instead of what I thought they needed.

The topic of "engagement" was hot at the time, but almost everything published was for major businesses or brands with a giant following. Hardly anything was available for those just starting out. I decided to create the book that would teach them how to build engagement even if they were starting from scratch. While I had ideas about how to solve this problem, many experts and authorities had more valuable perspectives. I solicited their views on the topic.

Now, as a rule, I hate compilation books, but this was the best answer to the questions my audience was asking. I put my own biases aside and created the book I knew people wanted to read. The result was *Engagement from Scratch!*, and unlike my previous products, it was built to deliver what my audience wanted, not what I thought they needed. I self-published it in November of 2011, and it became a runaway success. It has been downloaded over 100,000 times, has garnered over 200 reviews on Amazon, and was on the marketing bestseller list for almost two years straight.

As my writings reached more readers, I received more questions, comments, and feedback. By far, the most frequently asked question was about how I did so much guest posting. Now, I'd love to say that I quickly and cleverly saw this for the opportunity that it was and jumped on it... but that wasn't the case. The truth is, it took me months to notice the pattern, and months more before I stopped resisting (my focus still being on selling the doomed marketing training). I finally decided that if everybody wanted to learn how to do this, I would teach them. I tentatively offered a pilot program for this new offer, which I called "Write Like Freddy" (referring to my "Freddy Krueger of Blogging" moniker). To my great surprise, it sold out almost immediately—faster than anything I had ever sold before.

I delivered the pilot and gathered feedback from my students, which I used to refine my curriculum and roll out an updated version of the product. The pilot was sold in January of 2012. By the end of that year, almost a thousand students had enrolled in my program. Write Like Freddy was my first blockbuster success. It wasn't until months later that I looked back on the successes of *Engagement from Scratch!* and Write Like Freddy that I realized the common thread they shared, and that made them different from the ill-fated MaestroReading and ironically named Marketing That Works program: my failures followed the mainstream "build it first, sell it second" approach to business, whereas my successes were created by placing the audience first and using the process of co-creation.

And these two projects weren't just lucky flukes; they were just the beginning. I followed the same piloting process and built the Audience Business Masterclass, which has become one of the most successful courses in our industry. I created it the same way as I did Write Like Freddy: one step at a time, starting with a small, rough pilot, then gathering feedback, iterating, and finally launching the full course. When the launch dust settled, we had enrolled over 450 people. The total deal value of all those sales? $294,865 in just 25 days.

I was so busy doing the work and supporting my students that, for a while, I didn't even raise my head to look around. But when I did, I noticed something strange was going on: everyone who was successful with courses was following the same iterative process, but hardly anyone was growing as fast as we were – after all, going from zero to over a million dollars in just a few years is rare, especially for someone who was starting completely from zero – or rather, a quarter of a million dollars of debt below zero!

The piloting process was part of that trajectory, but something more was going on. We'd known for a long time that our students were engaging and succeeding in our programs at rates that were unheard of in our industry. I began to wonder, was that why we were growing so fast? It makes sense; if you sell better stuff, at better prices, and get people better results, then of course more customers will find you. But why were our students seeing such great results?

Sure, the solid strategies we were teaching were part of it, but there was more to the story: It was the information/education divide. There's a big difference between giving someone information and teaching them how to use it. And I have made it my personal mission to not just give my students the best information, but also to be with them every step of the way, lending my experience and expertise, to help them succeed. This was the real driver of the rapid growth of our business, because it was the reason our students were seeing great success.

I had found a real solution for regular people, like you and me, even complete newbies. When I found myself at a conference in the Philippines, talking to a gentleman named Nathan Liao about his accounting certification preparation business, I excitedly shared the strategy I had developed. We talked for an hour about how he could apply this same piloting process, laden with my education approach to business, to launch his first course. He thanked me for the advice, and I went back to my room. A month later, I followed up with him to see if he had applied anything we had discussed. He had, and the results were spectacular, bringing in over $5,000 in the first 24 hours, without even having built the product!

Emboldened by Nathan's success, I taught the process to

my private clients, and their results were nothing short of spectacular. Word quickly got out that my private clients were making impressive strides in their own businesses, and more and more people approached me, asking how they could do the same in their own businesses. At first, I tried to point them to resources, but there weren't any good options. Some of the information was good, but I just couldn't, in good conscience, endorse products that were merely *information* and didn't provide the support or outcomes of real *education* – not when I knew first-hand how much of our students' success depended on it.

And the few times I did point people to other resources, they wouldn't hear of it. After all, our proven reputation for making education programs was what brought them to me in the first place. That's when I started seriously thinking about building an education product to teach our course-building strategies. But first, I had to test the idea through... a pilot.

I was one of the speakers for the Superhero Summits, an event my friend and colleague Marisa Murgatroyd runs, teaching my ideas about building online courses. Then I invited people to enroll in a pilot course on the topic. Over 250 people signed up. The pilot gave me a chance to refine the ideas I was teaching, and more importantly, confirmed that people were interested enough to pay money to learn how to do this. That's when I made the commitment to dig in and build the Course Builder's Laboratory.

We tested our ideas, first in the pilot course, and then in a live four-day training to my private students, before we first launched it in February 2015. Hundreds of students signed up. It was our first million-dollar launch. We got to work supporting our students, and soon, they were succeeding in all niches and industries, ranging from health care, to relationships, to corporate strategy, to travel, and everything in between.

And as successful as the course had already been, we didn't rest on our laurels; we watched closely to see where our students struggled and continued to improve the course, to help them do better. It took us less than a year of piloting and iterating before we launched the second version of the Course Builder's Laboratory in the fall of 2015. It became our biggest, most successful launch to date, with $2.6 million in sales.

Because of the success of the Course Builder's Laboratory and many of its students, I decided to write a book about the opportunity in teaching online courses. The first edition of the book you're reading now, *Teach and Grow Rich*, shot to overnight bestseller status because the ideas resonated with many people. Within the first month of its release, it was downloaded over 14,000 times in the United States alone, and has since earned an average rating of 4.5 stars from over 200 reviews on Amazon.com.

Since then, a few people who've read the book have run away with the ideas in it and created their own online courses. Thousands more have become educator entrepreneurs with support from me and my team at Mirasee.

And that's how my Teach and Grow Rich story has become interwoven with the stories of people around the world who are seizing this opportunity. My hope is that the next one will be yours.

About Danny Iny

Danny Iny is the founder of Mirasee, host of the Business Reimagined podcast, bestselling author of multiple books including *Engagement from Scratch!* and *The Audience Revolution*, and creator of the acclaimed Audience Business Masterclass and Course Builder's Laboratory training programs, which have together graduated over 5,000 value-driven online entrepreneurs. He lives in Montreal, Canada with his wonderful wife (and business partner) Bhoomi, and their two children, Priya and Micah.

Made in the USA
Middletown, DE
26 April 2019